Agricultural Cooperatives of Colorado

- Blake Valerius -

Printed in the United States of America

First Printing, 2020

ISBN 978-0-578-72102-6

To anyone with a strange fascination,

May you also find a productive application

Acknowledgements

I'd feel remiss to not thank the University of Denver, particularly the incomprehensively massive and costly database and online resources that they provide me at my own dime. In all seriousness, I would have not been able to write this without the millions of articles, databases, search engines, journals, and other various sources that I had access to in order properly research for this book – all hidden behind a paywall that I would have to had paid for if the University hadn't. For example, a single outdoors industry analysis report used in this book would have cost me $925 to access at IBISWorld. After scoffing at my monitor and screaming into my pillow, I put a shot in the dark and Googled "university of denver ibis subscription" and found the link to the University's account which I have access. Indescribably clutch in the moment. Thanks, DU!

I'd like to thank my parents for the funding and encouragement, and all the cooperative leaders who spent their precious their day speaking with me – Agfinity in particular, who went above and beyond to give me a superstar treatment that I didn't exactly merit. I'm wearing the hat you gave me while writing this now.

Author's Note

Colorado agricultural cooperatives may seem like a dull subject, of this I am starkly aware, yet it isn't as much what they are that makes them interesting, rather it is more of what they accomplish. When surveying the US economy macroscopically, the cooperative business form seems like a strange abomination of confusing principles cast off to the side of relevance; after all, many of its tenants on the surface run opposite to the cutthroat competitiveness that the US economy is known for. At least, this is what I thought before I knew anything about them. Cooperatives are often unfamiliar and difficult to wrap your head around. So when I set out on my road trip across Colorado to interview as many managers and CEOs of agricultural cooperatives as I could, I didn't even fully understand what co-ops were or did. It was only after dozens of conversations that I came to see what, at the root, cooperatives are. If you wanted to make an all-encompassing, definitive statement about the cooperative business model, and be correct, I suppose you could say that cooperatives are sensible solutions to common issues among a similar people. If you have bothered to read the Author's Notes, which I, personally, rarely do, than I am going to reward you with a hint that will help you reap more from this book than you would otherwise. This book isn't about the Agricultural Cooperatives of Colorado as much as it is about how people who live in the same region and face the same difficulties can harness the free market of the United States with the power of their private finances to solve their shared issues with a solution optimized to their situation. Look for the *how* and the *why* in these recounts more than the *what* and the *when*, and you'll come away from this work with a head swimming full of ideas – cooperative solutions that you could see being beneficial to *your* life, regardless if it's an agricultural problem or not. I'm fairly convinced that every American has at least one problem somewhere in their life that starting a cooperative could solve.

This book is called "Agricultural Cooperatives of Colorado", a name picked very purposely; it is not "*The* Agricultural Cooperatives of Colorado" for a good reason – it does not feature *every* agriculturally oriented cooperative registered in the state, but it does feature most of them – and enough to encapsulate all the types of cooperatives. I avoided documenting cooperatives that are copies of each other. While each co-op is unique in its own ways, sometimes the list of differences isn't enough to write very much about. This is called "Agricultural Cooperatives of Colorado" because it features all the significant differentiations on the idea of an agricultural cooperative that are headquartered within the state.

Chapter 1

Agricultural Cooperatives

Though easy to overthink due to their obscurity in popular culture, news coverage, and everyday life, cooperatives account for some of the most simple and logical business models in a capitalistic economy. Whereas privately held corporations are steeped in deep industry analytics, complicated ownership, agency problems, pressures to expand, and other critical internal and external stressors, cooperatives are generally far more straightforward in their operation, purpose, benefactors, ownership, management, motives, intentions, and bylaws.

Cooperatives are old and important. Many of the large financial explosions which raised Europe out of the medieval age (now called The Age of Antiquity) slumps were supported by cooperative business models. The Dutch, for example, had their golden age during the seventeenth century, a few decades after the two largest sectors of their seaports, transportation, and warehousing organized into cooperative businesses.[1] Perhaps a more impressive example of the cooperative model is Switzerland. The core of past and present Swiss government, from the Old Swiss Confederacy in 1291 to the Swiss Federal Council of World War 2, and their famous quirks like loose banking laws and hard neutrality can be attributed to the

---

[1] Hugo van Driel and Greta Devos, "Path Dependence in Ports: The Persistence of Co-operative Forms," Business History Review81, no.4 (2007), pp.681–708.

cooperative federal structure under which their citizen-members choose to operate.[2]

The cooperative concept is similar to the concept of business in that there are so many variations and different approaches to the notion that describing them laterally, as to not exclude one variant, leaves a vast definition that is almost uselessly vague. The ICA, International Co-operative Alliance, formed in 1895, London, aims to be the voice of cooperatives worldwide and has the most exposure to the thousands of cooperative flavors, so is most qualified to define what the term means.[3]

The ICA states that "cooperatives are people-centered enterprises owned, controlled, and run by and for their members to realize their common economic, social, and cultural needs and aspirations."[4] Notice that this definition says nothing definite about membership, governance, industry, economic structure, financial sourcing, region, or size. These types of classifiers start to appear in definitions as cooperatives begin to be categorized by their specific purposes.

Classification in general has come under fire in the past decades, especially when it comes to classifying an individual person. Think of classification as putting things into bins. These bins are opaque and have tall sides; a person cannot be put into more than

---

[2] geschichte-schweiz.ch. (2004). The Old Swiss Confederacy. Retrieved from http://history-switzerland.geschichte-schweiz.ch/old-swiss-confederacy-1291.html.

[3] Ica.coop

[4] International Co-operative Alliance. (2018). What is a cooperative? Retrieved from https://www.ica.coop/en/cooperatives/what-is-a-cooperative.

one bin. Sex, race, gender role, and religious beliefs have been treated as classes in the past. Think of categorization as chalk circles. One can stand in a certain circle but can see the other circles and choose to move between them, or perhaps the circles overlap. These historically class examples have socially transitioned to be considered as categories due to several civil rights movements over the past sixty years, however this isn't to suggest that classes are becoming categories exclusively. In other instances, it's clear that what used to be categories are becoming classes. Political affiliation is an important and dangerous example of this, where the rise in political apathy due to the trend of running further left or right to impress one's voter base can be seen as the opaque edges of the class bins of "Left" and "Right" becoming higher and higher. Unlike society or politics, when defining a business the classifications and categories used are more static and the challenge becomes ranking titles by scope – classifications can it into larger categories, which then can fit into even bigger categories or classifications. The overall objective of this book is to introduce the variations of agricultural cooperatives in Colorado, and classify and/or categorize them into the models proposed by USDA economist Dr. Charles Ling.

The first challenge of sorting the agricultural cooperatives in Colorado is deciding what makes a cooperative agricultural. This was gone about in a few different ways.

Dr. Charles Ling, the economist who's work on the theoretical nature of cooperatives in the farming industry is central to this book, has a very practical definition of an agricultural cooperative. Dr. Ling uses a modified version of Ivan Emelianoff's 1948 *Economic Theory of Cooperation* definition of the business form – being that cooperatives are the aggregates of economic units.[5] Dr. Ling simply specifies further that these economic units are farms. Thus, Dr. Ling's definition of agricultural cooperatives is that they are aggregates of farms, or member-farms, as he commonly refers to them as.[6] This definition is useful in that it's a very specific classification of agricultural cooperatives from similarly structured businesses in analogous industries; the members of the cooperative are not individual people, but individual farms.

A drawback of Dr. Ling's definition is that it cuts off a few very important niches of cooperative business in the agricultural industry. Necessitating that the whole of agricultural cooperatives consist of member-farms excludes the fringe elements of the common agricultural industry in the US, not just Colorado, like the consumer base, the energy sector, and the finance sector.

USDA Rural Development supplies a much less academic, yet more practical definition of agricultural cooperatives. This federal department characterizes these economic aggregates by their core business activities instead of member classification. USDARD says that agricultural cooperatives "help... farmers and ranchers market their products and acquire farm supplies...and help meet many other needs, such as supplying electricity, telecommunications, credit and financial services, housing, food, hardware and building supplies,

---

[5] Emelianoff, I. V. (1948). Economic theory of cooperation: economic structure of cooperative organizations. Davis: Center for Cooperatives, University of California.
[6] Ling, C. (2012). The Nature of the Cooperative. The Nature of the Cooperative (Vol. 65, pp. 4–4). Washington D.C.: USDA Rural Development.

among other services".[7] This definition is more inclusive, adding supporting business partners in agriculture like electricians, communications, and financial services. Local credit unions are small cooperatives, but this clashes directly with Dr. Ling's proposal that members of agricultural cooperatives must be farms because credit union cooperatives primarily consist of individuals.

The USDA definition includes many of the fringe components of agriculture that Dr. Ling's definition excludes. Dr. Ling's definition, however, makes considering and sorting of individual operations clear cut and logically based. The USDA's idea that any co-op involved in supporting farmers, even in a non-agricultural capacity, can be considered as in the field of agricultural cooperatives is too inclusive and lacks a necessary cutoff that is the purpose of a definition in the first place.

The definition in this book for agricultural cooperative is an aggregate of economic units whose primary activities are directed at the agricultural industry. Now – to decide what makes an agricultural cooperative Coloradan.

There is an official agricultural cooperative list from the USDA called Directory of Farmer Cooperatives, which breaks down the contacts and industry tags of over 1500 cooperatives by state across the US.[8] The 19 cooperatives in Colorado recognized as belonging in the farming industry by the USDA were then cross referenced with the database on colorado.coop. For the throughout

---

[7] USDA Rural Development. (2019). Cooperative Programs. Retrieved from https://www.rd.usda.gov/programs-services/all-programs/cooperative-programs.
[8] Wadsworth, J., & Coleman, C. (2019, May).

readers who check the footnotes as they read, you might notice that this domain name is the same as ICA's domain name. That's because colorado.coop is the official page for ICA in Colorado.

On colorado.coop is a search function where dozens of cooperatives in Colorado can be found by location, name, or industry. Most of the cooperatives under the "Farming and Development" industry were very local: 1 to 3 locations exclusively in one region of Colorado. Others weren't – large businesses like CHS, who has hundreds of locations across the country, or Western Sugar Cooperative, a multi-state operation based off the intersection of Hampden Avenue and I-25 in Denver.

To be an agricultural cooperative of Colorado, you must be headquartered in Colorado. This removed a handful of ICA listed cooperatives who had locations in the state, but were large, multi-state enterprises based somewhere else.

Agricultural cooperatives can grow to be colossal. CHS Inc. is based out of Inner Grove Heights, Minnesota; they ranked 97th on the Fortune 500 in 2019 at $32.7 billion in revenue.[9] The second largest agricultural co-op, Dairy Farmers of America, isn't even half the size of CHS – at a measly $14.8 billion in 2019 revenue.[10] To put this into perspective, REI, one of the most well-known merchandise co-ops in the biggest outdoorsy cities of the country, did $2.8 billion

---

[9] Fortune Media. (2019).

[10] USDA Rural Development. (2018). Agricultural Cooperative Statistics 2017. Agricultural Cooperative Statistics 2017. USDA Rural Development. Retrieved from https://www.rd.usda.gov/files/publications/SR81_CooperativeStatistics2017.pdf

in sales in 2018.[11] The largest agricultural cooperative in Colorado is Western Sugar Co-op, with a revenue of $359 million in 2017. These certainly aren't your grandpa's small-town buyers' clubs.

Because cooperatives are funded by, operate for, and appeal to their members before all else, the amount of a co-op's sales can usually be depended on as a good reflection for the co-op's other sizes, both in the number of members and the physical regional spread.

Trends in the overarching agricultural cooperative industry are very consistent. Over the past decade, 60 agricultural co-ops have closed their doors each year. The total number of USDA-classified agricultural cooperatives in the nation has fallen from 2,475 to 1,871 since 2008.[12] This trend is interestingly identical to the fall in total agricultural co-op membership, from 2.351 million to 1.89 million over the same ten years, suggesting that the average cooperative that closed had about 770 members.

This isn't to mean that the industry is failing. The agricultural cooperative industry has gained 15,000 new full-time employees since 2008. This employee gain is happening at the same time that 60 cooperatives close, sell, or merge each year, which means that

[11] Recreational Entertainment Inc. (2018). 2018 Consolidated Statements of Comprehensive Income
Recreational Entertainment Inc. Retrieved from https://www.rei.com/assets/about-rei/financial-information/rei_fy18_issued_financial_statements/live.pdf
[12] USDA Rural Development. (2018). Agricultural Cooperative Statistics 2017. Agricultural Cooperative Statistics 2017. USDA Rural Development. Retrieved from https://www.rd.usda.gov/files/publications/SR81_CooperativeStatistics2017.pdf

the hiring rate in the agricultural industry is rising. In 2008, the average agricultural cooperative had 50 full time employees. In 2017, that number rose to 75.

So, while the agricultural cooperative industry lost 25% of its businesses, the number of the industry's full-time employees increased by 12.1%, and the number of full-time employees per co-op rose 50%. While looking at the trends in the number of businesses and employees is one way to judge the strength of an industry, it is a bit of a roundabout method when the change of equity and income in the industry could be used instead.

From 2008 to 2017, the total equity for USDA's agricultural cooperative industry rose 83.8% and the top 100 cooperatives saw a 103% increase in total income. These are incredibly strong numbers, making the decrease in membership confusing.

If cooperatives are funded by and operate for their members, shouldn't a decrease of nearly 20% in national membership damage the industry? Why isn't there more membership when the average return on member equity across the US was over 24% in 2017? Or might the high average return on equity (ROE) be exclusively attributed to the consolidation from the numerical decline of membership?

It's these oddities that make agricultural cooperatives such an interesting industry. There are an unaccountable amount of external and internal forces that have an impact on the entire business environment, right down to the level of a single operation in, say, the middle of Monte Vista, Colorado.

All of these mysteries are convoluted and certainly inter-linked with each other, as well as with the current events and trends of the outside world. To properly analyze and answer the questions posed in the past few paragraphs would take an entire book in itself. Instead, let's zoom back out. Why do cooperatives even exist in the first place?

Chapter 2

Choosing Cooperatives

If the concept of a cooperative still seems too theoretical or undefined, perhaps a story will make this business form appreciable.

One day, a coal miner in Pennsylvania gets fed up with his helmet. He's had gripes with the design and fit for some time now, which all boiled over when it came loose and drooped over his eyes in the middle of installing pipeline on the ceiling of a shaft, causing him to drop the pipe, ripping out several bolts where he had fastened it to the rocky ceiling previously. He aired out his frustration to a colleague, who echoed his sentiment. Curious about how many miners disliked the helmet which their employer supplied, he started asking around to anyone on the job he bumped into. He talked to his friends who mined with other companies and found that they, too, could find things that could be improved about their headwear. He talked to his boss, who in turn talked to his boss, who said new helmets weren't in the budget.

The coal miner relayed this back to the few people who were most passionate about finding a solution to this common problem. Instead of taking no for an answer, they decided to start a cooperative for Pennsylvanian coal miners who disliked their headwear. To join the cooperative, a miner would have to pay a flat fee, somewhere between $200-$400. In return, the cooperative would take into consideration that individual's chief concerns and spend the membership money on research and development. A year later, the cooperative of now 500 miners introduced its first model of their new helmet. Members of the co-op got the helmet first – at a reduced price. Miners outside of the cooperative could also buy the helmet at full price, least they decide to pay the $200-$400 to join the co-op. The cooperative also has the power to influence the various coal mining corporations which employ the co-op's members. While, originally, our coal miner's boss's boss said there wasn't money in the budget, to keep unions happy and their image positive they agree to partially split the cost of the co-op's improved helmets with new and current employees.

Ask yourself, why was a co-op the best way to tackle this problem? Why not a traditional business? What makes a co-op more attractive to 'investors'? What gives a co-op more influence over another corporation than a traditional business might have? Who wins in this scenario? After reading this book, you will see enough patterns of situations like this Pennsylvanian example to answer these questions with confidence.

Quite a bit of this book is going be spent describing the various business models, value propositions, key activities, customers, members, profitability, challenges, and partners of the agricultural cooperatives in Colorado. This is going to get really bland and uninteresting if you don't:

1. Know what a cooperative looks like in terms of members, governance, and goals.

2. Realize what a cooperative offers to stakeholders, which another form of business can't/doesn't.

3. Appreciate the creativity and flexibility that a cooperative can demonstrate to address the problems of its members.

To illustrate these points, we are going to begin with analyzing two non-agriculture cooperatives; the differences between them and between other traditional businesses in their industries will help you see smaller differences between the co-ops and traditional businesses in the agricultural industry later in the book.

REI

While Recreational Equipment Incorporated just might be the most wishy-washy name for an outdoors apparel supplier, it is the most prominent player in the hiking and outdoors industry, and one of the single most recognizably cooperative-modeled businesses in the nation. At $2.8 billion in revenue in 2018, it has just under 35% market share of the $8.1 billion hiking and outdoors industry. [13] [14]

It might be easiest to think the beginning of REI like the formation of the mining helmet cooperative. It began with one common problem that boiled over on a problem-solver. In 1935, ice picks cost Lloyd and Mary Anderson $20 per unit, the equivalent of $375 in

[13] Recreational Entertainment Inc. (2018). 2018 Consolidated Statements of Comprehensive Income
Recreational Entertainment Inc. Retrieved from
https://www.rei.com/assets/about-rei/financial-information/rei_fy18_issued_financial_statements/live.pdf
[14] Fernandez, C. (2019). Hiking & Outdoor Equipment Stores in the Us. Hiking & Outdoor Equipment Stores in the US. IBISWorld.

2020.[15] [16] This was due to middlemen in the US marking up prices from Austrian dealers. Fed up, and married to German speaker, Lloyd began ordering directly from the Austrians. Mary translated the catalogs and soon Lloyd was getting ice picks for $3.50, including trans-continental postage. The word spread to others in the Seattle climbing community, and everyone wanted in on the cheap prices. 23 people, including the Andersons, formed REI Co-op in 1938 in order to afford to front the costs of larger orders from the Austrians. The fee to join was $1, homage to the original principle of affordability.

In 2020, the main competition REI had is VF Corporation and Patagonia, both traditional businesses. VF Corp is a parent company for brands like The North Face, Smartwool, and Vans. Patagonia uses a premium price model and emphasizes longevity. REI stores sell both Patagonia and VF products, creating some sales overlap in the comparison between them. While REI does sell these types of products at high prices, REI's original principle, affordability, is still evident in their stores via their self-branded products. The "REI" branded products significantly undercut the same products of any other brand while keeping quality consistent.

Membership with REI has also kept with the business's founding principles. With inflation, the $20 lifetime membership fee is nearly equivalent in market value to the $1 fee in 1938. The $20 membership at REI gets a member 10% back on all full priced

---

[15] https://www.bls.gov/cpi/
[16] REI Staff. (2019, February 13). REI History: It Started With An Ice Axe. Retrieved from https://www.rei.com/blog/camp/rei-history-it-started-with-an-ice-axe.

products; it pays for itself in the first $200, which is the average price for a cheap family-sized tent. This 'discount' comes in the form of a member dividend.

Member dividends follow a similar procedure as dividends from stocks. At certain points of the fiscal year, be it quarterly or annually, excess profit from a business will be given out to the company's owners, the stockholders, divided up by a flat rate per stock. For example, if a company has 100 stocks and wants to pay $100 in dividends, each stock will receive $1 – if you own 40 stocks, you get $40, if you own 1 stock, you get $1. It's a bit different in co-ops. The distribution is not tied to the number of ownership stocks, but to the individual member's activity. Usually dividends will go back to the members in proportions to patronage, how much a member has spent or invested with the business in the latest financial period. This is highlighted excellently by REI's dividend model.

At the end of each year, 10% of what a member spends is returned to them via a card that works like a gift card. Don't want to spend your dividend at REI? No problem. You can redeem it to your bank account or walk into a store and leave cash in hand.

Cooperatives aren't legally required to give out dividends in the same way that other businesses aren't legally required to give out dividends on their common stocks. Even if REI didn't give out dividends, they still host a cohort of programs that justify the $20 lifetime membership, like a considerable amount of member-only coupons, free or heavily discounted classes in every outdoor activity, and cheap services on high maintenance products like bikes and skis.

REI will most likely never be usurped in the hiking and outdoor industry. The only business form that could compete with all that they offer would be another cooperative; the amount of revenue that REI invests in and gives back to its members is simply unsuitable for any for-profit business to match. Tax exempt nonprofits are legally unable to distribute profits to members or investors.[17] For-profit corporations might be able to redistribute profit to its owners, and nonprofits might be able to offer extremely affordable services, but only a cooperative can do both at levels significant enough to distinguish them from the other business forms in an industry.

HealthPartners

HealthPartners is the only significant healthcare 'cooperative' in the nation.[18] At a revenue of $6.6 billion coming into 2018, it was ranked as the seventh largest cooperative by revenue in the United States. They operate out of the Midwest from the Twin Cities, providing affordable health insurance, among other healthcare services, to its members.

Besides its isolation in a co-op-deficient industry, HealthPartners has one massive difference between itself and REI. One of the largest selling points for REI is that they're a cooperative; it's advertised on their website, in their logo, in their stores, and by the

---

[17] Tittle, C. (2016, November 30). How are nonprofits and co-ops different? Retrieved from https://cdi.coop/how-are-nonprofits-and-co-ops-different/.

[18] National Cooperative Bank. (2017). NCB Co-op 100 List. NCB Co-op 100 List. National Cooperative Bank.

cashiers asking if you'd like to spend the $20 for a lifetime membership when you check out. REI heavily embraces the cooperative image. HealthPartners does not.

The only place where HealthPartners identifies as a cooperative on its entire website is in its history section, where it mentions offhand that cooperative medicine was not legal before HealthPartners, and its founders spent 20 years working to change the laws before founding the company.[19]

Even then, in the section where they cover their formation in 1957, they refer to the business as "one of the first consumer-governed, prepaid health plans," seeming determined to avoid using the word "cooperative" at all costs.

A good explanation for this mystery is that HealthPartners is not, in fact, a cooperative. HealthPartners was founded as, and has always been, a nonprofit corporation.[20] The reason that it's considered a cooperative, and ranked amongst them by the National Cooperative Bank, who's NCB Co-op 100 List is the Fortune 500 of cooperatives, is because it has the bylaws of a cooperative.

Cooperative businesses can be filed with the states as such, but that doesn't stop a group of people from filing a business as a nonprofit and then governing it as a co-op. The biggest business reason to do this is the tax breaks.

---

[19] HealthPartners. (2019). Our history. Retrieved from https://www.healthpartners.com/about/history/.
[20] Office of Minnesota Secretary of State.

When co-ops don't plan on ever giving their members dividends or redistributing profit to them, it's economically favorable to take the tax breaks of a nonprofit, at the cost of doubling down on legally barring the business from giving money back to the members. Think of it as an ethical tax loophole. The business can still create bylaws that give members the same kinds of democratic powers that members of a co-op have, operate in their interest, and use common issues to attract, unite, and help members. Nonprofits can look exactly like a co-op, save having the ability to redistribute patronage.

The decision between which kind of filing, cooperative or nonprofit corporation, depends on which one the founders think will give the members the best economic high ground. The direct utility of profit to the members can be a strong deciding factor, and might not be in the form of cutting them checks.

In 2019, REI had 18 million members and in 2018 they paid $204 million to their members in dividends, an average of $11 per member. [21] [22] This is over 70% of REI's 2018 profit, so it's easy to see how much they embrace the cooperative model. The 30% of profit left over is spent on investing in local communities and growing the business. If REI were a nonprofit, what would they do with that 70% of profit that they are now unable to redistribute? They're a thriving retail store, and already the industry leader while only using under 30% of their profit to grow. REI can't serve the members best by growing the business at all costs, that does little directly for the

---

[21] REI. (2019). About REI: REI Co-op. Retrieved from https://www.rei.com/about-rei.

[22] REI. (2019). About REI: REI Co-op. Retrieved from https://www.rei.com/stewardship.

members; it best suits the members of the co-op to get that profit back via dividends.

HealthPartners had 1.8 million members in 2019, though the number of members has little to do with their better compatibility with the nonprofit classification.[23] The healthcare industry has a different focus than retail, their members care less about getting cash dividends back each year; they're looking for cheaper healthcare, and additional services. Any profit that HealthPartners makes does best for their members to go back into HealthPartners to improve their services through additional care like clinics and research, and extended reach; covering a larger region to offer membership to more Midwesterners.

A dollar in the hand of a cooperative might provide more value for a member than giving that dollar back to the member directly, as illustrated in this example between HealthPartners and REI. This is one of the main reasons why some co-ops give dividends and other don't, as well as the explanation as to why a co-op might file as a nonprofit when it knows that returning patronage will never make sense.

Traditional Business

The traditional goal of business is the same between a cooperative and a traditional corporation; maximize shareholder value. This is referred to as the traditional goal of business, Friedman's

---

[23] HealthPartners. (2019). Quick facts. Retrieved from https://www.healthpartners.com/about/facts/.

shareholder theory, because a handful of other business theories have cropped up over the past two decades, all more expansive and inclusive to stakeholders who are not shareholders.

While older, this classic shareholder theory is still relevant in spotting the largest difference between a cooperative and stereotypical businesses, that being the identity of the shareholders for which each is tasked to operate.

In October of 2018, Apple reported having 23,712 shareholders on record.[24] In March of 2018, Walmart reported having 229,858 shareholders of their common stock.[25] McDonalds reported having 1,781,818 shareholders in January of 2018.[26] There were 101.9 million iPhone users in 2018, Walmart sees 265 million customers each week, and McDonalds sees over 69 million people per day.[27] [28] [29]

This means that 0.02% of Apple's total iPhone users, 0.087% of Walmart's weekly customers, and 2.58% of McDonald's daily visitors are the people who these companies are in business to please. Apple is not chiefly concerned for 99.98% of its iPhone

---

[24] Apple Inc. (2018). Form 10-K 2018. Retrieved from SEC EDGAR website http://www.sec.gov/edgar.shtml
[25] Walmart Inc. (2018). Form 10-K 2018. Retrieved from SEC EDGAR website http://www.sec.gov/edgar.shtml
[26] McDonalds Corp. (2018). Form 10-K 2018. Retrieved from SEC EDGAR website http://www.sec.gov/edgar.shtml
[27] eMarketer, & Website (appleworld.today). (March 12, 2019). Number of iPhone users in the United States from 2012 to 2021 (in millions) [Graph]. In Statista. Retrieved from https://www.statista.com/statistics/232790/forecast-of-apple-users-in-the-us/
[28] Walmart Corp. "About Us." Corporate, 2019, https://corporate.walmart.com/our-story.
[29] "McDonald's - Official Global Corporate Website." McDonald's - Official Global Corporate Website, 2019, https://corporate.mcdonalds.com/corpmcd.html.

users, by the traditional business model, it sells iPhones to create value for only 0.02% of its users.

Most companies, albeit smaller than these three, have the same kind of ratios between the number of shareholders, people that it is responsible to create value for, and number of customers, the people who are directly involved with the services and/or products of the business.

In cooperatives, the majority of 'customers' are 'shareholders'. Even in retail co-ops like REI, who open their stores to non-members, 73% of its 2018 profits came from patron members, a much larger figure of shareholder participation than in Apple, Walmart, or McDonalds.[30]

This percentage of sales from members nears 100% as the industry get more refined, and a handful of specialized cooperatives only sells to members. In a produce marketing co-op for example, member-farmers sell directly to each other at lower prices because there is less risk when the products are certain to sell.

This relationship between being part-owner and customer isn't a sure thing in cooperatives. Some co-ops, especially marketing co-ops, exist so that a small number of member-producers can sell with the power and leverage of a larger corporation; in these, the customers are businesses or individuals who aren't members of the cooperative at all. This kind of business form still holds a special

---

[30] "REI Co-Op Announces Record Financial Results, Major Expansion of Rentals and Used Gear." REI Newsroom, 4 Sept. 2019, https://newsroom.rei.com/news/corporate/rei-co-op-announces-record-financial-results-major-expansion-rentals-and-used-gear.htm.

relationship between shareholders and the business that isn't as prevalent in non-cooperative corporations. In these marketing cooperatives, the shareholders become the suppliers instead of the members, a position that's just as important to the business as the customer base.

What makes cooperatives special is that the people they operate to create value for make up a much larger proportion of the number of people that the business interacts with than in for-profit corporations. Cooperatives are many times more dependent upon their owner base than other business types are – whether these owners are on the supplying or consuming end of the revenue stream.

Modern Business

Theories of modern business focus increasingly on maximizing value for all stakeholders, not just for the shareholders. One, plainly called Stakeholder Theory, was published in 1984 by R. Edward Freeman.[31] It details the interconnected relationships between a business and its customers, suppliers, employees, investors, communities and others who have a stake in the organization; anybody who can be impacted by the decisions of a company is a stakeholder, albeit at different levels of importance.

Cooperatives are also distinct in the eyes of Stakeholder Theory in that the members of a cooperative hold many more

---

[31] StakeholderTheory. (2018). About. Retrieved from http://stakeholder-theory.org/about/.

stakeholder labels than a customer or employee of another for-profit corporation might.

The amount of types of stakeholders could be broken down into as many as one would want to intricately analyze a business, but there are six types commonly addressed in corporate social responsibility models: customers, employees, investors, suppliers, communities, and governments.

Typically, a person who interacts with a business holds one stakeholder identity: customer, employee, investor, or supplier. A few hold two: an employee and customer, supplier and investor, supplier and customer, etc. A minority of a business's stakeholder might hold three: an employee, customer, and investor, or customer, supplier and investor. Communities and governments aren't individuals but groups of individuals with different relationships with a business.

In cooperatives, this is flipped. The majority of stakeholders in cooperatives hold 2-3 identities, and a minority of stakeholders have only one. To illustrate this best, take the previous section on traditional business where we saw that the majority of people who interact with a cooperative are shareholders, as known as, investors. Members of REI, HealthPartners, and CHS, pay an annual or one-time fee, an investment, to be a member, giving all members that shareholder identity by nature.

On top of the investment, these members will be a supplier or customer depending on the function of the co-op, bringing the minimum number of identities to two. In cooperatives where the members are primarily customers, employees will likely be a member as well, thus hold three identities, but this may not be true in a co-op where members are suppliers as there is a higher barrier of cost and skills required to be a supplier than a customer. Suppliers in marketing cooperatives might hold a position similar to employees in a retail co-op, being a supplier, customer, and investor. There are certain cooperatives, especially marketing ones, where some members are all four, investor, customer, employee, and supplier. An example of this will be seen later in the book.

Choosing Cooperatives

While there are many benefits created by the cooperative business form, they have down sides that typical for-profits and nonprofits don't. They're hard to grow, slow to change, and subject to prejudice.

The democratic process which governs cooperatives does a fantastic job of making sure all members are rowing in the same direction, but it tempers the rate that changes can be made, which may be detrimental in rapidly changing industries. Members holding out, particularly if that member is voted onto a board within the cooperative, can halt mobility in a way that a typical for-profit corporation would never experience. Some cooperatives wait for a unanimous agreement among members before any governmental decision is made, which would be a nightmare scenario for a typical for-profit company.

Growth is tricky, especially when the money used for growth comes directly out of any potential dividends. Thus, a balance must be struck between investing in the business and returning patronage to members; extremes of this balance were illustrated in the REI versus HealthPartners example. Another difficult aspect of growth is that most cooperatives are regionally based, meaning that they appeal to a certain customer in a geographical area. To expand the regional area of a cooperative, there has to be a potential member base already established outside of the current operating area. For example, HealthPartners began in Minnesota and over sixty years later, they've only expanded to five other states, the immediate neighbors of the home state. HealthPartners is famous with its members and doesn't give dividends so they don't have to worry about keeping a growth to dividend balance, yet despite their popularity and easy funding it's still difficult for them to expand any faster than the word of mouth of from their members and a limited advertising budget.

Prejudice is another environmental force working against cooperatives. Many cooperative managers have to fight the stereotype of being "your grandfather's business". Co-ops get misunderstood as being old-fashioned or a tight-knit club. This is typically a consequence of appearance; the storefront or website of some cooperatives seem like they're stuck in the 1990's – or earlier. They don't keep modern architecture, interior décor, or web design at as high of an importance as other for-profit companies do. This goes back to growth being tricky; updating appearance is expensive and cosmetic – it doesn't have as much utility as other investments might, yet it matters when attracting new, younger members, and combating the negative stereotypes around cooperatives. There is a dollar value for all companies when it comes to the effect of poor appearance on revenue.

Choosing between cooperatives and other for-profit and non-profit business types comes down to a net benefit when comparing the ability of the potential members to succeed in addressing their shared problem while facing the challenges that comes with cooperative business.

Rocky Mountain Farmers Union Cooperative Development Center

The Rocky Mountain Farmers Union Cooperative Development Center is a nonprofit offshoot of Rocky Mountain Farmers Union. It was founded in 1996 and has spent the last quarter century supporting emerging and pre-existing cooperatives and like-minded projects across Colorado, New Mexico, and Wyoming. They do this by playing a handful of roles.

First, RMFU facilitates the planning process. When an entrepreneur reaches out to them seeking guidance in starting an agricultural cooperative, often times they are not familiar with some or all of the path from taking a cooperative idea and turning it into an operating business. RMFU helps entrepreneurs by providing outlines, common practices, and past examples of startup cost estimates, ease of member recruitment, and general timelines.

In addition, RMFU estimates the feasibility of an entrepreneur's idea through environmental studies, reducing the chance of the founder hitting a dead end with their project. Once the feasibility looks good enough for serious consideration, RMFU works with the cooperative's founder(s) on developing a business plan to give clarity to what the cooperative is going to look like, and to make their idea marketable to prospective members and/or investors.

Next, RMFU advises the entrepreneur on how to develop the organizational organs of the co-op, and how to structure membership, including defining member roles, benefits, and theoretical capacity. This administrative development happens synchronously with fundraising, which is another activity that RMFU can assist with.

Since their first season in 1996, RMFU's Cooperative Development Center has received a Rural Cooperative Development Grant, a program funded by the USDA, every year. The Development Center has also received donations from their parent company's foundation, and from the Gates Family. RMFU gives money from these sources to promising startups, but they also function as a network for the entrepreneurs to find other sources of fundraising in private individuals and corporations, and with public local or state government programs.

Following the start-up, RMFU remains to be a valuable contact for the growing cooperative. Their advice and experience is used to help their client cooperatives face and overcome obstacles incurred as the business expands. Past the contacts at RMFU are the other clients of the RMFU, a community of all the co-ops that RMFU has helped. If the resources at RMFU are insufficient or inexperienced in whatever issue one client has, another in the community has most likely encountered a similar situation, and co-op-to-co-op cooperation happens through this network.

Since 1996, RMFU's Cooperative Development Center has seen the client cooperatives and other businesses they've worked with raise over $84 million in capital and have created or saved over 770 jobs. In the four years between 2012 and 2016, they've seen 16 agricultural cooperatives incorporated, and have assisted 57 others. Since 1996, they've formed over 120 cooperatives across the Rocky Mountain states.

A few examples of the agricultural cooperatives assisted by RMFU are Southwest Farm Fresh, High Plains Food, and Poudre Valley Community Farms, which are all featured in this book.

Key Takeaways

By keeping these in mind when you reach the chapters concerning the cooperatives themselves, it will be easier to understand the reasoning behind some of the decisions a co-op makes.

- Behind every cooperative is a group of people, the members, who decided to get together and form the co-op, and who contribute to the day-to-day business.

- Members can be the primary suppliers, primary customers, or both.

- Cooperatives use their profit to benefit their members. This can be in the form of giving back cash in proportion to a member's activity or investing it back into the co-op to expand the services it offers, or a combination of both.

- Most cooperatives are for-profit businesses – their profits are returned to the owners, who are the members.

- Cooperatives provide a range of benefits to their stakeholders that other forms of business are not able to match due to financial or legal restraints.

- Slow growth, sluggish change, and antique public image are difficulties faced by almost every agricultural cooperative.

- Cooperatives, especially agricultural cooperatives, are beloved and encouraged by all levels of the US government, and have access to an immense amount of state and federal resources.

Chapter 3

The Many Faces of Cooperatives

The Many Faces of Cooperatives is an article in the fall 2012 edition of the Rural Cooperative's Magazine.[32] It's written by Dr. Charles Ling, an agricultural economist whose work is renown within the Department of Agriculture and is the subject of study in this book. Dr. Ling wrote a series of articles about agricultural cooperatives for USDA Rural Development between 2006 and 2012. Dr. Ling retired in January of 2015 after 40 years of government service, most of it being spent with dairy cooperatives.[33]

In *The Many Face of Cooperatives*, Dr. Ling defines seven variations of the agricultural cooperative model, based upon "different commodities [having] their own characteristics, and different types of cooperatives [having] their own special features."[34]

These seven variations are marketing cooperatives, new-generation cooperatives, purchasing cooperatives, local-food cooperatives, multi-stakeholder cooperatives, farm production cooperatives, and cooperatives with non-patronage members.

The term Dr. Ling uses for classifying these, 'variation', is purposefully broad. While these terms are defined separately, and each have the word 'cooperative' in them, they are not stand-alone

---

[32] Ling, C. (2012). The Many Faces of Cooperatives. Rural Cooperatives, 79(6), 24-29.
[33] Campbell, D. (2015). Economist Charles Ling reflects on 40 years of changes in dairy co-op sector, 82(1), 12-13, 37.
[34] Ling, C. (2012). The Many Faces of Cooperatives. Rural Cooperatives, 79(6), 24-29.

terms. As discussed earlier, categories and classifications can be drawn from arranging these terms by scope and meaning. The agricultural cooperatives of Colorado won't only belong to one group exclusively; in many instances one co-op will embody parts of models across several of Dr. Ling's variations.

Marketing Cooperatives

Marketing cooperatives fulfill the role of advertising, promoting, and selling the products of member farms, also known as producing members, to non-producing members, locals in the community, and other grocery or food-processing businesses. They're like the salesmen for the producing members in their cooperative.

They allow for family farms or small operations to band together and compete against larger companies within the same industry while retaining that family-farm sensation. Oftentimes these marketplaces take the form of online pages and farmers' markets – occasionally a storefront. Marketing cooperatives can include delivery services to families, grocery stores, and restaurants in the region.

New-generation Cooperatives

New-generation cooperatives are referred to as such because they emerged in the 1980s and 1990s to address the trend of depressed farm income by offering value adding programs to capture processing margins for its members.

To offset the additional risk which the cooperative must undertake to provide this, new-generation cooperatives usually require a significant equity investment to membership and delivery rights, which ensures adequate supply is raised.

The delivery rights are preset so that there are limited uncertainties surrounding the volume of capital that will need to be processed, meaning that while the cooperative is owned by the members to add value to and market their products, the capacity which can be handled is limited. New-generation cooperatives are marketing cooperatives that process or augment their members' goods before selling them.

Purchasing Cooperatives

Your stereotypical Ace Hardware gas station combo, purchasing cooperatives are farm suppliers who use the equity of members to organize, purchase, and sell supplies and services, mainly to members. Think REI, but for fertilizer, engine belts, horseshoes, and overalls.

Some purchasing cooperatives who are either geographically desolate enough, or popular enough, open multiple branches across several farming regions in order to achieve economies of scale in sourcing major supply items, like storage, feed, and fertilizer.

Local-food Cooperatives

Local-food cooperatives have risen from the recent demand in locally produced food. These communities are usually geographically defined or are small rural regions selling to metropolitan areas. While they are technically marketing cooperatives, Dr. Ling specifies them as a unique variation because of the shared commodities and characteristics between them.

Multi-stakeholder Cooperatives

Multi-stakeholder cooperatives are comprised of businesses and individuals who have a stake in the local food chain. This includes growing, value adding, marketing, selling, and buying activities. Members of this variation of cooperative could be farmers, suppliers, marketers, truckers, or buyers. While the cooperative is overarching, each member typically stays in their field of expertise.

Farm Production Cooperatives

Multiple farmers can come together and pool resources in order to operate one or more farms. This form of cooperation allows an assortment of farmers to assemble and manage inputs at a level that wouldn't be practical for a single individual to undertake.

In farm production cooperatives, the most important cooperative aspect to refine is the channels of operation. The management of these businesses is most concerned with coordinating the members in their production responsibilities, so clear lines of expectation, roles, and authority are key to orchestrating a successful farm production cooperative.

Cooperatives with Non-patron Members

The difference between patron and non-patron members is intent. To patron members, the cooperative represents a solution to an issue in their life and they're going to use the power and services of the cooperative to improve their situation. To non-patron members, the cooperative represents a business they find valuable to the community or is bound to grow, so they'd like to invest some cash into it. Non-patron members aren't looking to use the products and services of the business, so they wouldn't receive dividends or discounts; non-patron members receive investment returns in proportion to their share of investment, and appreciating value on their original investment – assuming the co-op is growing.

The kinds of voting power and privileges of a non-patron member vary to the extent that a particular cooperative finds useful, and state government allows. Membership types can mix, a patron member may also invest in the cooperative, receiving the benefits of both a patron and non-patron member.

Cooperative Variation, Categorization, and Classification

Specifying these types of identifications and knowing which kinds of identifications apply to a cooperative is important for anyone who has stake in the cooperative market. Although it seems academic or theoretical, there are plenty of practical reasons to be able to talk definitions.

Knowing the variations of agricultural cooperatives helps when taking a new idea and turning it into a viable business. While many of these variations overlap or could be encompassed within each other, their existence helps in putting words and definitions to the initial idea, and also provides a source of precedent and inspiration in carrying out and expanding that idea.

Speaking to the preliminary members and stakeholders, registering with the Office of the Secretary of State, and writing the by-laws of the business are all made easier when a cooperative can be easily defined by assigning it these labels.

Cooperatives with similar structures also find commonalities between best business practices. These can be practices in structure, organization, governance, sourcing equity, and operation. Most variations of cooperatives share best practices in all of these areas of business, but there are unique differences between a minority of these activities that are central to how that minority variation works. For example, the structure of agricultural cooperatives are aggregates of independent agricultural economic units, except for in farm production cooperatives where the structure is of dependent agricultural economic units. Another example of this is that the governance of cooperatives with non-patron members are partly defined by individual state laws where the governance of the other variations are member-governed as dictated by the cooperative business form.

Identifying the best practices for whichever mix of agricultural cooperative variation a business holds allows managers to optimize the leadership of the cooperative. James Wadsworth is a program leader in education and member relations for the USDA Rural Development Cooperative Service. Part of the materials in education he has published includes an information report addressing cooperative directors about asking the necessary questions to yield the most valuable insights, which allows for better decision making at the top. The questions aren't applicable to all variations; a majority of questions only make sense to one or two of them at a time. If a manager knows the variations, categorizations, and classifications of their cooperative, they will be able to easily discern which questions are useful to ask, and which wouldn't make decision making any easier – there are questions for certain types of agricultural cooperatives which others wouldn't even have an answer to.

The real-life application of these theoretical identifiers won't fit the exact specifications of any agricultural cooperative; these businesses are much more complex than any umbrella-styled definition can fit. Trend identification via commodities and characteristics can be better used as a tool than a doctrine. If an agricultural cooperative has the commodities and characteristics of a marketing cooperative, the label of 'marketing cooperative' is more important in providing ideas of how to reinforce, maintain, and expand by presenting the trends of other 'marketing cooperatives' than for offering a dogma by which to operate.

Chapter 4

Purchasing Cooperatives

To most, the concept of a cooperative is the concept of a purchasing cooperative. Purchasing cooperatives, after all, are the oldest model of economic aggregation. A group of contemporary peers pooling resources in order to get access to better supplies, and/or getting cheaper rates for their supplies is a logical solution to their shared problem, and procuring supplies is a much older issue for farmers than distributing goods; for most of human history, people lived in low density villages and towns unlike today's urban preference. The first modern cooperatives were purchasing cooperatives. In 1844, 28 artisans in Rochdale, north England, began the Rochdale Equitable Pioneers Society in which they pooled their scarce resources to buy basic food commodities in bulk.[35] Members of the cooperative were able to buy those ingredients while earning dividends from the co-op whose size depended on how much they bought in a year. Another classic example of a cooperative, credit unions, share the same principles of purchasing cooperatives. The first credit union came about in Saxony in 1862 with the same member rights as the 1844 Rochdale Equitable Pioneers Society. The Saxons did not know of the cooperative in England; the idea of a cooperative business model was independently formed in both instances.

---

[35] History of the cooperative movement. (2020). Retrieved from https://www.ica.coop/en/cooperatives/history-cooperative-movement

Today, there are more marketing cooperatives in the US than purchasing cooperatives, the ratio is about 5:4, signifying how the issues contemporary farmers faced over the past 175 years have shifted to include distribution as well as the original issue of obtainment. While marketing-focused cooperatives are the hot new model of economic aggregation, purchasing cooperatives are still as vital and prevalent as they were in 1844; some of the purchasing cooperatives and ex-purchasing cooperatives in Colorado were founded closer in time to the Rochdale Equitable Pioneers Society than the birthdates of the people who now run and own them.

Monte Vista Cooperative

Monte Vista Cooperative Association began in 1949 by a group of forward-thinking farmers who wanted to pool resources in order to buy farm supplies in bulk. Since their opening, MVC has expanded tremendously in membership and buying power.

In 2019 their number of voting members, who are required to file Schedule F forms with the IRS, was just shy of 1,700. They also had about 3,200 members who are referred to as 'participating patrons' that still receive dividends on their patronage and other member perks but cannot vote because they aren't farmers.

They have expanded on addressing their initial issue by increasing the variety and stock of products and services offered exponentially. MVC provides fertilizer, fuel, seeds, crop treatment, feed, hand tools, tire and vehicle services, clothing, hats, and other hardware products through their storefront in Monte Vista. Their power as a purchaser has enabled them to partner with businesses from all across the United States in order to provide more exclusive farm equipment like planting and harvesting machines from Minnesota, portable flex hoppers from Kansas, and tractors from Texas.

This is what Eric Hinton, the President and CEO of MVC, says sets them apart from your average ACE Hardware or smaller purchasing cooperative. MVC addresses many areas of farming activity under one roof, and at the added benefit of patronage refunds.

"We like to think we're held at a higher standard because we're owned by our members; that they expect the best of the best, along with a good price."

-Eric Hinton, President and CEO

MVC primarily serves the San Luis Valley in southern central Colorado, though the local highways allow them to serve out to Salida, Gunnison, and Creed – an area of over 3,000 square miles.

Retaining membership through the cycles of generations and providing to both small and large producers are the largest challenges MVC faces.

MVC believes that the biggest misconception about agricultural co-ops is that they're "your grandfather's business or your father's business". New millennial farmers aren't considering membership with co-ops because they want to go try something new that's different than what they watched their parents use growing up.

Millennial farmers in the San Luis Valley think that MVC is out of date and that their practices are antiquated because of their long history, despite MVC offering the most advanced brands of equipment and product in the valley.

The concerns of a lifetime farmer with a massive operation and a smaller hobbyist who grows for their family are worlds apart. MVC needs to know the chief concerns for each party and provide products carefully tailored to challenges faced by each; keeping the large producers in the forefront, as they have more interaction with the cooperative, while not letting the smaller producers drop into the rearview. Most non-cooperative business wouldn't attempt this; they'd choose to target one or the other because of the differences in needs. MVC undertakes the challenge because local farming is important to them, at all levels.

MVC says that about half of their members fully understand what distinguishes them from a non-cooperative business, with a small proportion on or close to the company board of directors knowing exactly what makes their business model unique, and another small proportion on the opposite side of the spectrum who have no clue what a cooperative really is.

One of the reasons half of their farmers may not fully appreciate the cooperative business form is because unlike REI, MVC doesn't pay out equity on a member's patronage until the member is 65. What this means is that while a member at 20 years old will be receiving refunds based on their purchases at that age, MVC won't pay those refunds out, in the form of ordinary income, until that member turns 65.

Because MVC is involved in so many lines of farming operations, they have incredibly strong lines of competition in certain areas, and next to none in others. These competitors are both multistate chains and local small businesses. In addition to MVC in the fertilizer market, for example, there are two local competitors, a regional competitor, and one international seller in Monte Vista. In petroleum, there is also a mix of a global name and local independents.

In the 21st century, the largest change to the farming supply market is the speed of supply and service. With the rise of efficient farming due to technology, along with the trend of consolidation within the US which sees the number of farms slowly drop while acreage rises, the ability – and necessity – for a farmer to plant fast and with abundance has increased. The ability for a farming supply company to keep up with these new demands is the key to keep the business of farmers.

Growers want the right price and fast service. They're willing to pay MVC premium prices to take good care of them out in the front of the growing season, because the timeliness of their crops is the most important factor to them. Farmers want to come in and always see the products in stock, which puts MVC in a tricky situation in maintaining inventory levels during the seasonal intervals in such an isolated part of the state while not being overstocked with product they won't be able to sell, as supplies like fertilizer can't be hedged against in the future. Their members want MVC to have the right equipment and the right people to get it done at the right time.

When looking into the future, the largest factor limiting growth is the water crisis which has stricken the San Luis Valley over the past decade. Implications from state directives on water pumping and water rights has led to a shortage. The resulting impact is a 20% reduction in acreage over the past 10 to 15 years, and it's forecasted to happen again in the next decade. MVC will see a reduction in input demanded because of this loss of acreage, so they'll require a plan to stay fiscally viable. Hinton predicts that MVC's present level of diversification will allow them to absorb the downturn.

The cost of being a cooperative for MVC is primarily in administration duties. Bookkeeping for each member's equity and patronage returns, answering to a board of producers who each have unconscious personal motives in decision making, and attracting young customers are all difficulties which MVC wouldn't face if it were a private business.

Over the 70 years it has been in business, Monte Vista Cooperative has become an important part in the season-to-season operations of over fifteen hundred farmers in the San Luis Valley. But the farmland is drying up, the corporations are moving in, and the new millennial farmers are apathetic. MVC has overcome every obstacle so far, yet to take on three challenges at once – MVC must evolve by 2030 or else its high-water mark could be behind it.

Poudre Valley Cooperative

Poudre Valley Cooperative is a single-location operation just off of, and visible from, I-25 as the freeway cuts through northern

Fort Collins. All of the purchasing cooperative's departments work out of this plot, which is surrounded by manure-scented farmland. For all the purchasing cooperatives who make their identities by using their buying power to source the products of dozens of brands under one roof, Poudre Valley Cooperative takes the alternative route of using their power to harpoon a few whales; private franchises.

PVC began in 1947 on the outskirt of oldtown Fort Collins. In 1976, the location moved 4 miles due east, to its current location off the interstate. It now offers hardware goods from their Ace store, and gasoline from their Cenex pumps to over 3500 members across Adams, Boulder, Larimer, and Weld counties.

Franchises are stereotypically thought of as fast food chains, which are normally owned by a managing family – a private individual who contracts with the franchise. Gas stations are distributors that use partnerships between the gas parent company and another business, a convenience store for example. This is done because both parties operate in different industries with different key players, meaning for either to take on both functions would require them to have expertise in two separate trades. PVC franchises with Ace and Cenex for the same reason a convenience store would partner with a gas company or a private individual a McDonalds. PVC has the land and the customer base, and Ace/Cenex has the product and the supply lines. Put them together, and you've got all the basics needed for profitable business. They're symbiotic relationships – everyone wins. Cenex and Ace get access to a preexisting customer base, they save on marketing, they don't have to build or lease a development, and they don't have to pay employees outside of transporting their products to the storefront. In return, PVC gets to offer trusted name-brand products while being able to make a killing by buying their Ace/Cenex supplies in bulk.

One of these two kinds of partnering is more prevalent than the other; it is much more common for a purchasing cooperative, especially a well-established one, to partner with a fuel provider than a hardware provider. The reason for this is that by the time a cooperative has the customer base and fiscal ability to franchise with a hardware store, they've already accumulated a plethora of buying contracts with suppliers, whom with they often have long standing relationships. While it may be easier, and cheaper, to cut the majority of buying contracts in favor of one large hardware franchise, being able to pick and choose between brands and makers across different hardware departments gives the cooperative the ability to optimize their product offering to their member's taste. When a purchasing cooperative gets large enough to require a greater and more consistent volume of supply, or their desired product offering becomes more diverse, this is when they will cut ties with the many individual suppliers in favor of one large supplier i.e. Ace. PVC is an example of this, but so is Agfinity – which is one of the largest cooperatives in the state in terms of revenue. The small size of Colorado's average agricultural purchasing cooperative, however, makes hardware franchises a rarity. The majority of purchasing cooperatives aren't big enough, in terms of membership and membership need, to require switching to a franchiser. This is not the same for fuel.

Unlike hardware goods, if a purchasing cooperative is going to offer fuel it must come from a branded wholesale distributor contract. Gasoline companies are not technically franchises; the difference between a franchisee and a branded wholesaler is complexity of the relationship. The branded wholesaler simply buys the product from the producer and resells it under the producer's brand while a franchise relationship is a little messier. This simplicity is certainly a motivator for agricultural purchasing cooperatives to offer gasoline. Cenex is not only a preferred supplier to all Colorado co-ops, but is perhaps the single greatest example of cooperative to cooperative business across the nation.

Among agricultural purchasing cooperatives in Colorado, Cenex is so often the preferred provider of fuel that the gas company has a practical monopoly. There are multiple reasons for this, but one interesting aspect about Cenex might provide a singular explanation. Cenex is owned by CHS, which is the largest cooperative, agricultural or otherwise, in the United States by a margin of 18 billion dollars.[36] Cenex has been a part of, and has grown with, CHS since it was founded by the massive cooperative in 1931.[37] CHS is so large that Cenex is the fifth largest propane supplier in the United States.[38] This cooperative-based gas company has a great reputation with purchasing cooperatives all across the country and understands them, their members, and their function better than any corporation could. Even if the distribution deals with Cenex are only marginally better than a deal with another gasoline supplier, over the

---

[36] National Cooperative Bank. (2019). NCB Co-op 100 List. NCB Co-op 100 List. National Cooperative Bank.
[37] CHS Editorial Team. (2019). About CHS. Retrieved from https://www.chsinc.com/about-chs
[38] LP Gas. (2019, March 20). 2019 LP Gas Top Propane Retailer rankings - top retailers. Retrieved from https://www.lpgasmagazine.com/2019-lp-gas-propane-retailer-rankings/

last 90 years providing Cenex gas has simply become the thing do to, the industry norm, for purchasing cooperatives.

Purchasing cooperatives exist on a scale of size and complexity, with small barn house operations like Rocky Ford Growers Cooperative on one end, and the massive powerhouses like Agfinity on the other. Poudre Valley Cooperative exists as a fantastic example of these two worlds overlapping. It has the single-plot feel of a rural co-op while offering the name brands of an industry leading titan. The longevity of this limbo status is uncertain, but fun to hypothesize about. The next step for PVC would be for them to open a second location, but with the steadfast expansion of Agfinity Inc, which is approaching if not already on top of PVC's territory, this is easier said than done. Can PVC spread across the region, or continue their hold on Fort Collins, despite Agfinity's continued growth? If not, does that spell the inevitable, eventual end of PVC as their members splinter off to the competitor? It will certainly be interesting to watch this dynamic play out over the next couple decades.

Producer's Co-op

On the stretch of highway 50 between Telluride and Grand Junction is Montrose and Olathe, neighboring towns that are the home of Producer's Co-op, where popcorn and coffee are always fresh and free. It serves the ranches and farms of the Uncompahgre River valley between the peaks of the northern West Elk and southern San Juan mountain ranges. Over 1,600 members out of Montrose, Gunnison, Delta, Ouray, and San Miguel county belong to, what seems like, this small-town cooperative.

Producer's serves the +2,000 square miles of their membership spread from a pair of retail stores and services stations that lie 12 miles apart. To address the distances, they offer delivery on all products. These products are typical agricultural cooperative supplies like animal feed, farm and ranch hardware, and clothes, but also animal health supplies, like vitamins, vaccines, antibiotics, nutritional supplements, and medications, which aren't as commonly found in agricultural purchasing cooperative.

Producer's has been in the community for over 90 years, and contributes to seven banquets, events, and programs throughout the year in Montrose and Olathe. Like Poudre Valley Co-op, Producer's Co-op is a rural, small-focus business that has become an engrained pillar in the local farming community over successive generations.

Basin Co-op Inc.

Basin Co-op began in 1952 Durango 1952 Durango had a population around 7,500 and was hardly the tourist hotspot that it is today. Today, everything has grown. The population is closer to 19,000, tourists pour in and out of the southwestern Colorado town, and Basin Co-op has flourished. Their main location is just off the main highway, clearly visible to anyone going west on 160.

Basin Co-op is a purchasing co-op and offers the goods and services that is typical of a Coloradan agricultural purchasing cooperative. While they aren't unique in providing fuel, Basin Co-op is especially considerate to market their fuel transportation services. That may have something to do with their seven propane and refined fuel trucks – expensive investments for the co-op. These trucks carry propane, Cenex propane, to their members across southwest Colorado. In addition to delivery, budget billing and MR MAX propane contracting are other services offered by Basin Co-op that stimulate their sale of over 6 million gallons of refined fuel annually.

Basin Co-op Inc also offers a AAA-style service for tractors and trucks. They specialize in tires and batteries and host a full selection of passenger vehicle and pickup truck tires. Their service truck fixes industrial tires on-site. Unlike northeastern Colorado or the San Luis Valley, farmland in southwestern Colorado, especially around Durango, is incredibly decentralized in relation to the municipalities. Thus the fact that Basin Co-op has the capacity to bring their co-op and its services to their members is one worth advertising to the dispersed farmers of the region.

Unfortunately, Basin Co-op is a fantastic example of the stereotype that co-ops are old and out of touch. Their website is a relic of the 20th century. This stereotype is one of the largest obstacles, if not the largest in some cases, that co-ops have to continuing membership with young farmers and agriculturalists. Cosmetics has become an incredibly important feature to attracting millennials to brands. There are no brands, in or outside of agriculture, that have success with millennials if they seem even slightly old and outdated. 'Dropshipping' proves this beyond a reasonable doubt.* Out-of-date

---

* Dropshipping is a business model where cheap, poorly advertised goods are purchased in bulk by a dropshipper, who then lists them on a beautifully created, fantastically marketed, highly sophisticated website

websites makes a company seem untrustworthy, neglectful, or suggests that it is performing poorly. In the 21st century, the perceived sophistication of a company is directly correlated with the sophistication of that company's website.

What's interesting to observe about the southwestern Colorado co-ops is that, regardless of cooperative model, they converge towards tackling a regional dilemma: the distances between farmers, towns, and customers. In evolutionary biology this concept is called convergent evolution, when two different species that live in a shared environment evolve similar structures independently of each other; think bird and bat wings. The same idea applies to businesses. The two southwestern Colorado co-ops covered in this book are Southwest Farm Fresh Co-op, and Basin Co-op. There're 45 miles between them, and may have never heard of each other, yet their value proposition to members and customers have both independently developed to tackle the regional challenge of a decentralized population.

Agfinity

In 1905, 20 potato farmers formed a business to procure supplies and market their produce in Eaton. The farmers adopted cooperative-like bylaws and pooled $2,000, $100 per member, a $2.9k investment in 2020 USD. This business, the Potato Growers Company, pre-dated legal cooperatives in Colorado; the Colorado

---

for a significant markup. It's essentially a markup for a more aesthetically pleasing online shopping experience. The website itself adds value to the product.

Assembly didn't pass the State Cooperative Law until 1913. The Potato Growers Company reformed after 10 successful years in 1915 into the Potato Growers Cooperative. They, and their now 500 members, celebrated by building a new warehouse and elevator in Galeton, giving them two locations of operation. Through ups and downs over the next 50 years, Potato Growers Cooperative changed their name to Agland in 1967 in order to reflect the expanded range of crop products and services offered, and the progressive vision of the business. The next name change wouldn't be for 45 years when Agland Inc. and Brighton-based American Pride Co-op merged in 2012.

In 2019, Agfinity was the second largest Colorado cooperative by revenue at $226 million, though was undoubtably the single most important agricultural cooperative in the state. Every year, they send out three to four thousand member billing statements, indicating their amount of active member base. In the first six months of 2019, Agfinity distributed nearly $3 million in patronage refunds and equity retirement to their members.

They have members in Colorado, Nebraska, Kansas, Utah, New Mexico and Wyoming, though their primary artery of activity is up and down I-25 in Colorado. Membership at Agfinity is straightforward; Common members pay $250 to join and do not get to vote, Preferred members pay $500 to join and have voting rights within the cooperative. The difference in membership lies in the extent of financial dependence on agricultural activities of the member. In 2019, about 600 of the three to four thousand total members were Preferred members, and 400 of those were active in voting on cooperative affairs. Agfinity encourages the business of non-members, as do most purchasing co-ops, because they're the most likely market segment to become members.

Agfinity's rich history helps to pull back the topsoil and see just how deep their roots are interwoven in the agriculture industry of Colorado. In 2020, those roots helped to support six separate business departments that are complex enough to be their own entities entirely. These departments, feed, agronomy, fuel, tire & service, retail, and Colorado Commodities, each aim to fulfill the needs at every stage during a farmer's annual growing cycle. In 2019, they focused on expanding crop inputs and improving their marketing services. A June partnership with Answer Plot, a business specialized in capturing and analyzing the explicit metrics of successful crop inputs, tested a local swath of land in Gilcrest to ensure that Agfinity is offering specialized data for crop inputs in the north eastern Colorado region. Colorado Commodities is the alias for Agfinity Inc's marketing division. Colorado Commodities buys member's grain and ingredients, picks up the inventory from member's farms, and sells the product to an end user, typically as feed. Agfinity owns a mill in Eaton where they process this raw crop into an Agfinity-branded feed.

Because of Agfinity's diversification, they don't have any single major competitor. The agricultural landscape of Colorado is incredibly desolate when compared to Minnesota, Wisconsin, Illinois, or other midwestern states, so there isn't much competition for Agfinity's departments from other Colorado cooperatives. For the departments which are in highly competitive markets like feed, fuel, retail, and agronomy, the competitors are largely isolated to a single product market and are mainly private companies. Agfinity's physical reach, experienced operations, and membership benefits are enough to distinguish them from private competitors to anyone with a large enough farm operation to consider membership. That is to say, while certain business lines of Agfinity may face competition, the cooperative as a whole does not. The unsaturated cooperative environment in Colorado gives them a run on the market of potential members but makes growth via acquisition scarce. Agland was a titian even back before the 2012 merger with American Pride; Agfinity's relationship to the other agricultural cooperatives in Colorado, save Western Sugar, can be best illustrated as a big fish a large, sparsely populated pond.

The primary growth for Agfinity must be organic. Programs like Colorado Commodities are perfect examples of how Agfinity has gone about growing organically. Organic growth is typically riskier, more time consuming, and more expensive than acquisition, yet it puts Agfinity in full control of the expansion and gives them fantastic positioning to capitalize on success within the ventures once they become profitable. Co-ops are often thought of as uncompetitive, apathetic to growth, and not profit driven; this is not true. Being as money-hungry as for-profit corporations are is in a co-ops best interest because it increases the financial benefit of the co-op to its members. For example, if Agfinity doubles in profit while the number of members they have remain the same, then the size of patronage refunds or dividends could theoretically double. For example, the co-op can now afford to refund members 20% on their purchases instead of only 10%.

Growth is just one of the many challenges that Agfinity shares with other two-hundred-million-dollar businesses, another is sufficient staffing. Agfinity's 'corporate office' has recently moved from Eaton to Loveland, in a building right off I-25. As the cooperative grows, it becomes harder and harder for them to source and retain talent, especially if a co-op is headquartered in the middle of rural Colorado. The move to Loveland allows Agfinity to be closer to the talent pool of the metropolitan areas, Loveland is between Fort Collins and Denver, while keeping the view on the horizon of sprawling farmland, and a focus on their mission to help farmers feed the world.

The Future of Purchasing Cooperatives

Predicting the future of a cooperative is as simple as analyzing the problem it was created to solve. Purchasing cooperatives are formed provide its members, who often live in low income rural areas, access to better supplies at lower prices.

REI, for example, was formed because climbers in Seattle wanted to get high quality ice picks at a cheaper price from Austria. In 1938, this required a business to facilitate: you needed someone who spoke German, you needed regular catalogues coming in from Europe, you needed dependable delivery of the items and secure transfer of payment cross-continent. It was an undertaking that the only the administrative power of a front office in a proper business could handle.

If we teleported those climbers from 1938 to 2020, or we teleported 2020 technology to 1938, would REI ever exist? Buying in bulk from foreign countries is something nobody bats an eye at these days, you can do it from Alibaba on your phone. The potential REI founders might find it easier to buy their picks from Austria online, then use a referral program with their fellow climbers to get better prices, no cooperative organization needed. The exponential increase of globalization, effective communication, and efficient transportation has solved many of the issues that a person might have considered forming a purchasing cooperative to address fifty years ago.

It is a little different with agricultural cooperatives. These co-operatives have additional circumstances – after all, getting a ship-ment of ice picks from Austria online to a group of climbers in high-density Seattle is easier logistically then distributing pallets of ferti-lizer to 120 farmers across a couple hundred square miles. Unlike the REI example, if we teleported the founders of Agfinity to 2020, they'd still find reasons to begin the cooperative. They wouldn't have as many reasons as they did in 1905, but there are still critical func-tions that agricultural purchasing cooperatives fulfills for a modern farmer. The questions is: will the trend of slowly diminishing reasons to start an agricultural purchasing cooperative effect their prevalence and performance? Or are there fundamental utilities of an agricul-tural purchasing cooperative that will never be provided for by an ad-vancing world?

Recent trends could point to a dreary future for agricultural purchasing cooperatives. In the world of agricultural cooperatives, there are a few different important trends. The total number of co-ops is decreasing year to year, but marketing cooperatives are de-creasing in numbers by ~3% annually while maintaining growth in to-tal gross revenue, and purchasing cooperatives are decreasing in numbers by ~6% annually, while also shrinking in total gross revenue.[39] This suggests that marketing cooperatives are condensing, through mergers and acquisitions while growing economically and purchasing cooperatives are simply going out of business.

It isn't that simple. That purchasing cooperatives are failing is just one of the many explanations for the trends, and in many cases it isn't true. The largest purchasing cooperatives in the US consistently grow their annual revenue, and there are a few up-and-comers who are growing explosively, like United Farmers Cooperative from Iowa, and South Central FS, Inc. from Illinois, who both doubled their revenue between 2016 and 2017.

However, there have not yet been any new agricultural purchasing cooperatives in Colorado in the 21st century. Is this because Coloradan farmers already have all the purchasing cooperatives they need, or is it because there are now better ways to solve the issues that purchasing cooperatives once addressed?

Dr. Ling's Definition

Monte Vista Co-op, Basin Co-op, Poudre Valley Co-op, and Producer's Co-op all fit USDA economist Dr. Ling's definition of a purchasing cooperative because they are local, supply items at a retail level, and carry production supplies, farm, and home items. Dr. Ling specifies between purchasing cooperatives by breaking them

---

[39] USDA Rural Development. (2018). Agricultural Cooperative Statistics 2017. Agricultural Cooperative Statistics 2017. USDA Rural Development. Retrieved from https://www.rd.usda.gov/files/publications/SR81_CooperativeStatistics2017.pdf

down further into the goods they supply; cooperatives like the 1844 Rochdale Equitable Pioneers Society sold consumer products like food ingredients, meaning they'd be classified as a consumer cooperative, and cooperatives that supply loans, who operate with the same doctrine as a purchasing co-op, are classified as credit unions.

The reason Agfinity does not fit Dr. Ling's definition of a purchasing cooperative is because it is too large physically and more advanced in what it offers to its members. Agfinity once was a co-op that focused on purchasing supplies for its members but has grown so many additional lines of business that to put it in the same box as Poudre Valley Co-op, or Basin Co-op would be misleading. Agfinity better fits the description of a supply cooperative, which is a broader definition into which purchasing cooperatives belong. In supply cooperatives, purchasing commodities to sell to members is *a* business activity, but it isn't *the* business activity like it is in purchasing cooperatives. Supply cooperatives still sell farm and house products in a retail style like purchasing cooperatives do, but they also offer complex labor-based services that purchasing cooperatives do not. Many purchasing cooperatives offer services, but it's often on a small scale and a perk of doing business with them, like delivering products to member's houses, or servicing machines they sell. Supply cooperatives like Agfinity have large departments dedicated to labor-based services that have no direct relation to their retail, like Colorado Commodities, which is a subsidiary of Agfinity that buys and sells member grain, agronomic consulting, which analyzes a farming member's soil conditions and reports on how to best grow crops, and application services, which gives members the option of having Agfinity handle the fertilizer application on their farm.

Becoming a supply cooperative like Agfinity first requires success as a purchasing cooperative. A purchasing co-op can start the transition by investing to create new service-based departments in their co-op themselves, or by acquiring a nearby company that already does the services they look to offer their members. Both decisions require a fair amount of capital and financial stability, which is why many purchasing cooperatives never accomplish it – or take several decades to do so.

Based on my research, the purchasing cooperative that is currently in the best position for expanding the service side of their business and joining Agfinity as the second Coloradan supply cooperative is Monte Vista Cooperative.

Chapter 5

Marketing Cooperatives

Marketing cooperatives fulfill the issue of advertising, promoting, and selling the products of member farms, also known as producing members, to non-producing members, locals in the community, and restaurant, grocery, or food-processing businesses. They're like the salesmen for the producing members in their cooperative.

They allow for family farms or small operations to band together and compete against larger companies within the same industry. Oftentimes these marketplaces can take the form of online pages and farmers' markets – occasionally a storefront. Other marketing cooperatives can include delivery services to families, grocery stores, and restaurants in the region.

Marketing cooperatives are the predominant type of agricultural cooperatives in the United States, outnumbering supply-oriented co-ops by a ratio of 3:2. A good way to remember the main difference between a marketing cooperative and a supply/purchasing cooperative is that supply/purchasing co-ops sell *to* their members while marketing co-ops sell *for* their members. This salesman-supplier relationship can take one of two routes; the marketing co-op can buy its member's goods then sell to a third party, or the marketing co-op can facilitate the shopping place where it connects third party customers to members. The difference is whether the co-op uses its funds to buy their member's products, like a middleman, or the co-op sets up a marketplace where a customer buys from the producing member 'directly'. This same distinction is what roughly divides most marketing co-ops into two sub-types: New-generation and local-food.

It is rare to find a marketing cooperative that isn't new-generation or local-food. To operate a system where the co-op connects members to customers, then runs the logistics of facilitating a transaction, there has to be a limit on the geographic scope of member distribution. This is why it's called local food. It becomes inconvenient for the member, co-op, and customer if any one of the three doesn't live in the same region as the rest because the cost of the transaction increases, the time spent on logistics soars, and the food is oftentimes perishable. The solution to this, people realized in the late 1900's, is for the marketing co-op to buy the raw products from its members, and then sell them to the customers of their choice on their own terms. It is a good solution, but it creates a problem that the co-op didn't have before. When the co-op was the facilitator of the transaction, it didn't matter how much their members sold because the co-op worked off a percentage of sales. They didn't have any equity invested; they didn't have a dog in the fight. Their members could sell as much or as little as they wanted – it didn't impact cooperative finances. Now that the co-op was buying from its members and selling to a third party, their financial stability depended on the consistent supply of product, meaning that if each individual member was still able to decide how much or little they wanted to grow for the co-op, it would put the co-op into a state of omnipresent, everlasting, crippling uncertainty. The solution to this problem is an agreement. Before the growing season begins, the member agrees on an amount that they will supply the co-op that year, and the co-op guarantees to buy the agreed upon volume, often times down to an exact price. This agreement works well both ways because it solves a point of uncertainty for both parties. The member is guaranteed a buyer at the end of the season if they invest in growing a crop, and the co-op is guaranteed a certain volume supply from that member to sell to a third party. These agreements are often called 'delivery rights', or 'preferred shares', and correspond to an amount of land; one delivery right or preferred share would represent a certain number of acres agreed upon. This way, a member can adjust how many acres they want to supply the co-op by controlling how many delivery rights they own.

New-generation cooperatives use delivery rights, but it isn't just the delivery rights that defines a new-generation co-op. A new-generation co-op also has value-adding processes in order to increase their profit margin between transactions; they're not just re-selling their member's raw product at a slightly higher price – they add value to the raw materials, oftentimes transforming them drastically.

Finding a marketing co-op that doesn't fit the description of a local food or new-generation is rare because these two models of marketing are logical ways of doing business, and are widely applicable to situations where farmers need to market their products. Yet there are the few exceptions – including agricultural marketing cooperatives in Colorado that do not fit perfectly into either category.

Flagler Cooperative Association

In 2003, two agricultural cooperatives, one farm supply, one grain and feed, merged into Flagler Cooperative Association. Stretching the 35 miles between Limon and Flagler in central eastern Colorado are seven locations that make up the Flagler Cooperative Association. Four of FCA's locations, and all situated west of Flagler, are elevators. In agriculture, elevators, or grain elevators, are mechanical buckets or conveyors that carry loose grain into a storage facility, often a silo or a 'wheat bin'. This pair, the storage unit and storing unit, are combined into one term 'elevator'. The main function of an elevator is to store large grain quantities in a central location. While elevators are relatively recent – a product of the industrial revolution – the concept of stockpiling grain is almost as old as agriculture itself; granaries preserve the grain from moisture, allow societies to better combat shortages, and give governments the power to manage the food supply - for better or worse.

Elevators can come in a variety of capacities. The silo associated with the elevator can range from a family-farm size to rows and rows of large silos at a corporate farm. The reason this distinction is important is because it shows that the size of a harvest yield isn't a problem that would require an elevator cooperative to fix. Cost of construction and upkeep, and off-farm transport are more problematic aspects of private elevators, especially for small to moderate sized operations. Buying and building a private elevator, no matter how small, requires a certain fixed cost of time and money. They also require annual upkeep and depreciate just as fast as other farming equipment with lifetimes of about 20 years, according to

Professor Luke-Morgan at the University of Georgia.[40] The tradeoff of ownership is that a farmer gets to have complete control of when they bring their grain to market, but that brings up the second hardship for private operations – transporting the grain. Elevator cooperatives dilute the expense of elevator installation and upkeep per member and absolves the need for the member to coordinate transporting their grain to market on their own. Flagler Cooperative Association, as with all elevator cooperatives, addresses these by offering 'public' (to the cooperative members) elevators, and a cooperative coordinated-and-paid-for transportation network.

The other three locations that FCA has are in Flagler itself, a small town with a population of about 550.[41] One is an Ace Hardware (see Poudre Valley Cooperative section on Ace Hardware) another is a Country Store Express, and the last is the co-op's main office, and an additional grain elevator, both on one parcel of land. About 550 voting members make up the producing body. These are Schedule F, which is the tax reporting for farmers, producing members that are involved in the grain economy of the business; there is also a participating patron membership variation that offers dividends on money spent with the cooperative, be it at Cenex, Ace Hardware, or somewhere else.

While their elevators are more or less centralized, FCA's region of operation is anything but. In 2019, the area that their feed

---

[40] Hollis, P. (2018, December 14). Consider all costs of on-farm grain storage. Retrieved from https://www.farmprogress.com/consider-all-costs-farm-grain-storage

[41] US Census Bureau. (2017). Flagler, Colorado. Retrieved from http://www.city-data.com/city/Flagler-Colorado.html

sales covered was over 10,000 square miles - nearly all of middle eastern Colorado from Colorado Springs to Keenesburg, to Wray, to Wild Horse.

Competition and expansion for FCA are closely related in the sense that the most effective competition strategy is expansion through acquisition. Similar businesses to FCA in the eastern Colorado region are private companies in Stratton and Siebert to the east, and Anton Cooperative Association to the north. If FCA were to attempt an expansion into these areas, they would take the route of bidding to buyout the competitors (and their customers) versus going into direct competition over member loyalty. FCA keeps steady finances, maintaining a 30% debt to equity ratio over recent reporting history. This habit is what allows the fiscal strain of acquisition to be possible for what otherwise seems to be a modest rural small business.

Common risk factors for FCA are not so different from those of any agricultural co-op, particularly a sensitivity to weather, global trade, and politics that is more acute than in other industries. For Flagler, however, they have an additional strain that other agricultural cooperatives, or businesses in general don't. The unemployment rate in rural communities has dropped so low over the past decade that expanding, or even maintaining, business activity becomes difficult. For example, FCA began and ran a convenience store and automotive repair on the south side of town. In recent years, they've been unable to fulfill staffing requirements to the extent that they've either ceased operation or transferred management. The difficulty of finding employees in the area is an additional reason to concentrate on acquisition versus opening new locations as there's no guarantee of a workforce existing to operate a new location – why not just buy a workforce?

FCA is best illustrated as an iceberg; it doesn't look like much on the surface, but beneath the water is a massive operation and financial potential that makes the surface portion seem deceptive. The main office has the size, layout, and overall feeling of your rural grandparent's American Foursquare. The structures behind it are white silos built in the 1950's. Buzzing about, coming and going from the elevators, is a fleet of trucks that drive the primary business activities of Flagler Cooperative Association.

Western Colorado Beekeepers Association

The beekeeping industry is best summarized in the short conventional saying as overlooked and underappreciated. Unlike the large conspicuous effort of a crop farm or ranch, the physical presence of the operation of a beekeeper, as well as their livestock, isn't something you can usually spot from your car as you drive past.

Western Colorado Beekeepers Association formed in April of 2011 with 20-25 members. The issue that it formed to address was the lack of a network for beekeepers, both hobbyists and professionals, across the western slope of Colorado.

In 2019, they had about 75 members, 40-50 of which are consistently active within the cooperative. Of the members, 80% are hobbyist and the remainder professionals. The difference between hobbyists and professionals is amount of time spent and money made doing beekeeping with professional, or commercial, beekeepers having the majority of their income coming from bee-related activities.

WCBA's region is central western Colorado. Their territory stretches from Fruita to Edwards, and down to Ouray; about from Grand Junction to Vail to Telluride, to put it into popular perspective. Decisions within the cooperative are made by board members during monthly meetings. These events are open to the public and are the best place for members to exchange information, tips, tricks, and advice with each other. There are formal presentations put on by the co-op to address common issues that members will face in the coming month, such as swarm handling, honey extraction, and winter preparation.

WCBA thinks of themselves as a club more than a business. WCBA most resembles a marketing co-op but selling member products is only a portion of the marketing and advertising they perform. Since 2011, WCBA's function has expanded from being a network for contact to a network for action. In 2019, their most important purpose was the wide array of different types of community outreach that they're involved in every year.

Palisade's Honeybee Festival, Fruita's Farm & Ranch Day, UTE Water's Children's Water Festival, Tri-River Colorado State University's Demonstration Day, and Grand Junction's Animal Care Fair are sponsored and/or attended by WCBA. The stands at these events can be hosted by individual members, or the co-op as a whole. At WCBA stands, the primarily goal is education. Beekeeping equipment, samples of wax and other bee products, and lots and lots of fun facts and statistics are displayed on the tables. WCBA also puts on small seminars at a few of these events about the basics of hobby beekeeping and other interesting topics relatable to the general fairgoers.

Their website and Facebook pages are also troves of information. WCBA aggregates resources about beekeeping and bee products to serve their members and the local community. The facts that they provide are meant to help in decision making, not as rules to live by. This is one of the challenges that they come up against as an information provider. With the politicizing of certain aspects of the agricultural world can come accusations of biased news reporting. The facts and information that WCBA posts on their site and Facebook pages are just that – facts. The cooperative stays on the fence opinion-wise with issues like GMOs or pesticides, they simply provide the information and let members draw their own conclusions.

Another unique function that the cooperative model helps bring to the business is their swarm hotline. WCBA beekeepers across the Grand Valley will respond to honeybee swarms in the areas so that the general public doesn't have to handle removing them. Without the cooperative, contacting beekeepers to handle honeybee swarms would be much harder as there would be no centralized line of communication, which would leave the public to handle the swarms, and the honeybees to the wild where the survival rate of hives is only 10-15%. WCBA beekeepers attempt to save these bees.

Actual business transactions are rare for the cooperative. The network allows the members closest to the swarm to learn about, prepare for, find, and handle the honeybees in a timely manner. WCBA instead plays the role of facilitator, aggregating sellers of beekeeping equipment for members to choose from and providing a network of customers as physical and online traffic to members who sell bee products.

The equity payments for joining WCBA are more like club dues than they are patronage investments. The funds of WCBA are spent on business upkeep and community outreach instead of on the marketing and distribution of a centralized product pool like you would expect from a typical marketing cooperative. They try to keep costs as low as possible to maximize the impact each dollar from members can make on the community. For example, a member of the cooperative is a hobbyist, but has the full-time job of a CPA and does WCBA's taxes for free. Since the founding in 2011, some members have tried to change WCBA into a nonprofit in order to avoid taxes altogether, but the vote always ran to stay as a cooperative. WCBA doesn't pay out dividends, thus it is economically in their favor to be a technical nonprofit like HealthPartners, but the member's adherence to the cooperative business form is a testament to the power of identity that members feel towards their cooperative. WCBA members would rather pay a few hundred in taxes every year as long as they could keep themselves a true cooperative at heart.

At its core, Western Colorado Beekeepers Association is a marketing cooperative, but they do not market products. WCBA markets information, both within and outside of the cooperative. Whether it is the half-dozen links to beekeeping suppliers on their website, a presentation on winter hive preparation during a monthly meeting, or an infographic about the decline in honeybee population on a table at a fair, WCBA's marketing of bee-related information is the invaluable product of their business, and is what makes them an important agricultural cooperative in Colorado.

Why Don't These Fit?

Most marketing cooperatives in the United States fall into the categories of local-food or new-generation because these models are practical and widely applicable. Exceptions to this rule appear because the two subcategories aren't practical or applicable in every situation. Take WCBA, a cooperative whose focus is marketing, yet the business doesn't receive revenue from third parties because what they market is free information. In both local-food and new-generation cooperatives, the main source of income for the co-op comes from doing business with a third party. When there is no income from a third party, there is no reason to be a local-food or new-generation cooperative.

FCA's status as a marketing cooperative is a matter of comparison. Grain elevators like FCA can have tremendous success as a new-generation cooperative. Processing their member's grain into a higher value product can be an incredibly lucrative activity for an elevator co-op. FCA has preferred shares, which means they use delivery rights, so they have one half of the qualifications to being considered as a new-generation cooperative. FCA also has some value-adding practices. They mill a proportion of member grain into specific types of animal feed, which results in *some* of their products offered to third parties having an added value past physically mixing and packaging raw materials from members. This might be enough to consider them a new-generation cooperative if they were the only grain elevator cooperative in Colorado, but they aren't, and the other major grain elevator in Colorado is so deeply involved in value-adding processes that it makes FCA's partial milling look like hobby.

FCA is more new-generation than not, but when compared to the new-generation grain elevator cooperative Roggen Farmers Elevator Association, their lack of complex processing is magnified as a major difference between them. FCA is in the marketing cooperative section because its value adding isn't as pronounced, frequent, or as transformative as RFEA's value adding is.

Dr. Ling's Definition

USDA economist Dr. Ling's ideal marketing cooperative example is a dairy coop that sells member milk. This is the perfect example of a marketing cooperative that sells to a third party but doesn't belong to local-food or new-generation categories because a milk marketing cooperative can have the delivery rights of a new-generation, but lack any value-adding like in local-food – it's milk. Milk is the perfect product for existing in the limbo of the marketing cooperative realm because the profit margin between cow-owning member and milk-consuming buyer exists in the ability to package and sell it in bulk, and not from the ability to add to its per-unit value – milk goes into the cooperative, and milk comes out. Finding a commodity to replace milk in such a scenario becomes difficult to imagine having success with in the real world because the value between member and buyer must come from aggregating, packaging, and delivering the commodity and not from transforming it, or else it would become a new-generation cooperative.

The applicability of Dr. Ling's definition of marketing cooperatives to Colorado's one true marketing cooperative, WCBA, isn't perfect because WCBA doesn't market an agricultural commodity that can be consumed as energy, but an agricultural commodity that can be consumed as information. Dr. Ling does not specify if agriculturally-related information fits the definition of an 'agricultural commodity', which he uses in his description of a marketing cooperative.

Chapter 6

Local-Food Cooperatives

Local-food cooperatives have recently risen from the reinterest in consuming food products that are made or grown within the geographic vicinity of the consumer. For thousands of years, local food was the only kind of food humans ate. For most of American history, citizens ate local food because it was the cheapest and easiest to access. The Great Depression kicked off a swing in the balance of power between local farming and corporate farming. In the 1930s, thousands of acres worth of small farms were foreclosed upon by banks, lenders, and insurance companies. That land was liquidated by the financial institutions in mass auctions; the buyers were among the first corporate farms in America. Since the 1930s, the food industry has been dominated by large corporations whose ability to process a variety of grocery products in massive bulk has undercut the competitive edge that local shops once had. In the 21st century, a resurgence of interest in eating locally has enabled an aggregate of small, local farmers to find a market in which to sell.

Local-food cooperatives are meant to reestablish the marketplace that once existed between a region's residents and its agricultural producers. That marketplace is now typically online. Local-food cooperatives work by having the producing members list the products they offer on the co-op's overall store page, which is purchased by non-producing members, restaurants, and non-members. The co-op offers the storefront website and handles the logistics of transporting the product from the producing member to the customer and getting the money from the customer back to the producing member.

A unique feature of local-food cooperatives is that they do not use delivery rights. The transaction of money in a purchase with a local-food co-op goes from the customer to the cooperative to the producing member; the co-op earns revenue by taking a small percentage of the sale. In a co-op with delivery rights, there are two separate transactions: the member does business with their co-op, then the co-op does business with the customer – the member and customer do not interact. The lack of delivery rights in a local food co-op means that a producing member can sell as much, or as little, as they want. If there's a poor growing season, they won't be in hot water with the co-op for deficient production, and if there's a great growing season, they can set aside as much product as they want for personal use, then sell the rest through the co-op. The drawback to this arrangement is the lack of guarantee that a member will sell a certain amount. If a producing member wants to sell 500 bushels of apples in a year, but co-op customers only buy 250, that producing member is left with the bill for the 250 they didn't sell; if there were delivery rights, the member would be contractually obligated to produce 500 bushels of apples, but they would also be guaranteed to sell all 500 bushels.

Another feature of local-food cooperatives is that the goods they offer are often unique to the region and are difficult to sell in bulk. New-generation co-ops earn profit from processing raw materials, so they attract producing members that only focus on growing raw material. In local-food cooperatives, the individual members themselves may produce raw materials, but they will also add value to what they grow before posting it on the co-op's marketplace. If a family farm grows apples, they may sell the apples raw, but they're also likely going to make and market apple butter, apple sauce, apple cider, and baked apple products through the co-op. Some local-food members don't produce raw materials at all. Instead, they buy raw materials and transform them into marketable goods like soap, coffee, and toothpaste. The majority of products on a local-food co-op's catalogue have had value added to them by the producing member.

Pay attention to the dates that these local-food cooperatives began, and you will see how they emerged with the growing interest of eating locally/organically. Let's take a trip to small-town Colorado.

Southwest Farm Fresh Cooperative

In 2013, a roundtable discussion of community farmers decided that the greatest need they shared was for markets in the area. Located deep in the southwest corner of Colorado, near the border with New Mexico, their farms are as remote from a large city as possible, making identifying and reaching enough markets to sell off their inventory very a challenging task.

Farming is a full-time occupation, but so is the amount of work needed to form the relationships and implement the logistics of bringing their products to market. Southwest Farm Fresh Cooperative was formed to address this need by providing the relationships and logistics required to transport member goods to market in this isolated area.

In its infancy, Southwest Farm Fresh Cooperative worked with Local Food Logic, a private business that was also attempting to resolve the same issue. The two businesses eventually became one when SWFF absorbed the private company in 2014 to centralize the supplier and buyer networks.

In 2019, SWFF had close to 20 member farms that provided vegetables, fruits, herbs, beef, lamb, pork, chicken, cheese, and microgreens – among other seasonal products. People in the community can purchase 'harvest shares' or buy wholesale, which provides them deliveries that contain the goods from a variety of farms. The harvest shares are like claims on a consistent supply of food from a harvest. Their fall harvest share, for example, contains vegetable, cheese, meat, and ferment options. Each option is like a subscription to two month's worth of goods from the share for which they signed up. SWFF's wholesale model is a long-term delivery service for restaurants or households that want a consistent supply of locally grown food. SWFF supports this through their company refrigerated delivery truck, which travels from Cortez to Durango and Telluride to distribute wholesale shipments to cafes, restaurants, and resorts.

The area, though, is a challenge to the co-op. The drive from Durango to Telluride is 110 miles and over two hours, putting significant wear and tear on their truck and its volunteer drivers. Reaching further territories would mean doubling the miles and hours spent on weekly deliveries should SWFF choose to stay headquartered in

Cortez, which is closest to the greatest concentration of their farming members.

Weather has also been an increasingly damaging challenge for the business. 2018 saw extreme drought, which limited the volume of production for a majority of the co-op's farmers. 2019 was a high-water year, yet the cold spring season, including a freeze on summer solstice, killed off much of the crop. The cold-wet combination in the first half of 2019 brought in new diseases to the Four Corners region for the second half of 2019.

When everything runs smoothly, however, SWFF fully maximizes what a cooperative business model can offer. Because the issue the cooperative was formed to tackle was proposed by the farmer members, the level of responsibility and amount of activity that their members display is as high as a co-op can ask for. Some of the newer members who weren't at the roundtable to develop the mission of the co-op don't fully understand what makes SWFF different from another form of business. The leadership at SWFF is aware of this and seeks to get all members on the same page regarding the cooperative principles. One method to achieve this goal is their volunteer program. In order to cut administrative costs and keep membership fees low, SWFF requires that farmer members contribute time towards assisting with weekly tasks like packing or delivery driving. General manager Kendra Brewer says that after volunteering or going on ride-alongs, farmers come back with new insights into the business or suggestions for improvement, and a renewed sense of community between themselves, the co-op, and their markets.

SWFF's biggest competitors are traditional food distributors like Shamrock. The price and convenience that these massive corporations have conditioned SWFF's target customers to expect aren't realistic for what a local food cooperative can provide. The co-op can be impacted by regional weather conditions that don't affect large distributors, and the corporate prices are impossible to match. Instead, SWFF depends on their nature as a local food provider to differentiate their product and prices from large food distributors. In the local food provider market, SWFF competes with sizable single farms who aren't part of the cooperative but can compete at a lower price because of subsidies they receive from their tax classification. They also have to compete against similar local-food cooperatives when serving the tourist towns of Telluride and Durango.

The next steps for Southwest Farm Fresh Cooperative lie in expanding their ability to directly reach families. These kinds of programs are called community supported agriculture, CSA, and are exemplified by services like 'harvest share'. Selling to families or food pantries provides more of a community feeling for the farming members than selling to cafes or restaurants, not to mention that it isn't challenged by their geographical isolation as would expanding their wholesale delivery service.

High Plains Food Cooperative

Like many geographical features around the world, the High Plains food shed is not contained by political boundaries. The High Plains are a region in the western Midwest distinguished by the flat grasslands located along the far half of the slope from the

Mississippi river to the Rocky Mountains. If the political lines of the US states were reshaped to include the High Plains within a single territory, that state would undoubtably be named Flyover because that's what the High Plains are, the poster child for the US's most unremarkable terrain. Yet this isn't to suggest that that the people, businesses, or ideas in the High Plains reflect the region's bland features, and the High Plains Food Cooperative is a fantastic example of why.

The first major player in High Plains Food Cooperative was Chris Sramek, who led the charge for the creation of this business from a small western Kansas town – a whole 220 miles away from the heart of HPFC's core customer base in the Denver metro. Although Mr. Sramek's residency is ambiguous between his Kansas egg operation and his Coloradan co-op, HPFC is a true Coloradan business – conveniently based within a mile on the Colorado side of the Kansas-Colorado border. This split between Kansas and Colorado gives the cooperative a solid base in its name. The ~230 mile latitudinal spread of its producers encompasses a large portion of the High Plains food shed and gives the business the same sort of sprawling feel of the region itself.

Since late May of 2008, HPFC has grown in its operation size, member base, and progressive governing policies. One of the primary differences between Coloradan local-food cooperatives is their membership policies. HPFC breaks its customer base into two categories, wholesale and non-wholesale. Restaurants and grocery stores makeup the majority of wholesale clients, whose larger consistent orders provide the co-op a dependable stream of cash, assuming the co-op is able to provide a dependable supply of product.

Non-wholesale customers are households that order on an individual monthly basis. Membership costs $40 annually and is available to households and businesses in return for discounts on purchases and full access to HPFC's +700 item online store. Businesses are not required to be members to buy from HPFC unlike households, who need a membership to continue purchasing past the first two or-ders. These +700 items, while in stock, are delivered monthly to 13 delivery sites across Kansas and Colorado for households to pick up, and delivered to wholesale customers directly.

On the other side of the business are the producers. Over 50 family farmers across Kansas, Colorado, and Nebraska provide the goods that are listed on HPFC's impressive online marketplace. Joining as a producer costs $100 and gives a farmer voting rights within the cooperative, and access to over 300 household buyers and 10 wholesale clients – given that you first spend some time vol-unteering at a drop off site. Like many other regional agricultural marketing cooperatives in Colorado, HPFC does not have employ-ees and uses volunteer power to truck their orders throughout the High Plains. In order to avoid contention between the cooperative and its members, prices of products are set by the farmer selling the good. HPFC doesn't haggle these prices, which leads to occasional frustration for the co-op; giving farmers fair prices by allowing them to set their own has the potential to stall the business's finances if the prices are too high.

The producing members of HPFC have a good understand-ing of the benefits that their cooperative business brings them, but their customer members don't understand the pathway behind the household-to-farmer connection enough to appreciate the fine mechanics that goes into sustaining it. HPFC thinks that their customers would value their products more if they knew what went into their receiving of them – specifically the path from online store, to farmer, to pick-up site.

The most crucial part of this process is called last-mile distribution and is one of the central issues that HPFC initially formed to confront. With such a spread out region like the High Plains food shed, single family farms could figure how to get their products all the way to a concentrated customer base, yet it was that final mile between arriving to town and selling to a business or household that gave them the most trouble. Last-mile distribution is a common issue marketing cooperatives form to address, but what makes HPFC's case special is the distances that a farmer in Kansas or Nebraska has to confront to reach a market. Last-mile distribution is a bigger problem for a single family farm if it's the 201st mile versus the 21st, bringing about the largest operational difference between HPFC and another Colorado cooperative with a similar business model, like Southwest Fresh, that difference being the scope of operations that HPFC has managed to grow to and sustain. Through the selling power of a cooperative, which is comprised of a large product offering and a centralized sales force, and the delivery ability of cooperative, which comes in the form of branded refrigerated trucks and volunteers to drive them, HPFC confidently reports that they have solved the last-mile problem that has past plagued many High Plains farmers.

Perhaps the most impressive aspect of High Plains Food Cooperative isn't what they do, but how they do it. HPFC is doubtless the most progressive agricultural marketing cooperative in Colorado in their policies, governance, and long-term goals.

In order to become a producer of HPFC, a prospective member must adhere to 13 values and principles that include self-help, solidarity, democratic member control, and concern for community. An applicant must also pass an in-person site inspection of their farm by other producing members before being admitted into the organization. Governance of the cooperative is especially unique to HPFC. While all cooperatives are democratic, decision making in a democratic organization can be structured in different ways. Some co-ops use the majority opinion of voting members to make decisions, others appoint a certain number of representatives to vote for them, and others elect a board of people to make all management decisions. High Plains Food Cooperative is not just a true democracy, but a unanimous one. This means that if there is even a single vote among patronage members that isn't a yes or abstain, a change will not be made. An obvious con of this decision-making process is that changes cannot happen swiftly. On the flip side, consensus voting allows every member's voice to be heard and taken into consideration.

It's these kinds of open-minded policies that Emerald Gardens, a mircogreens producer, loves about High Plains Food Cooperative. Made up of millennial farmers, Emerald Greens has found a role within the co-op as a source of new perspective for other members; millennials and microgreens have both only recently emerged in importance. The progressive culture of the cooperative was what attracted Emerald Green, and the value system, marketing abilities, and community member leadership positions are what keeps the young farmers engaged.

A key enabler of the overall way HPFC functions is the complete lack of competition. Because Colorado produces so little produce, most of the produce consumed comes from out of state. With the increasing popularity of 'real food' and eating locally, what little produce grown in-state typically sells instantly, so long as it can reach market. The customer targeted by out-of-state distributors isn't the customer targeted by HPFC; HPFC isn't in direct competition with massive produce corporations. This means that the more HPFC grows in membership, the larger market share of the local-food industry they capture, and the likelihood of a similar cooperative cropping up in their operating territory as a competitor decreases – so long as they keep the farming members satisfied.

The result of these securities is the option for High Plains Food Cooperative to operate at their leisure and take risks. One example of their progressively inspired risk taking is a venture into Aurora. Aurora is the largest and most diverse municipality in the Denver metro region yet is overlooked when it comes to local food. It is on the eastern border of the metro, meaning it is at the tip of the western edge of the High Plains. Setting up a food hub in the city would be a complex undertaking for the eastern-Colorado based business, including the accumulation, transportation, and warehousing of goods, marketing and marketing research for the food hub location, and staff to operate it. The time and money required to bring this vision to fruition is on par with the greatest tasks that HPFC has completed to date, yet with the support and ingenuity of their diverse member base, it is hard to image the cooperative failing or backing down from a challenge.

Fresh Food Hub Cooperative

Along the main strip of downtown Norwood is a blue house with a red door, the storefront of the Fresh Food Hub Cooperative. Inside are rows of metal wire shelves stocked with local meats, treats, produce, and other random items. It's just like any other small foody pantry, but the people working it, supplying it, and profiting from it are members of a cooperative.

Traditionally, members of food aggregate cooperatives tend to be farmers. Marketing, especially in isolated areas like Norwood, is a challenge for small producers and family farms. Co-ops are then formed around that shared frustration, so that customers may find all of their regional growers in one centralized place. Purchasing cooperatives are the opposite of this, customers are the ones looking to aggregate products to buy, and they form a cooperative to do that. Fresh Food Hub has many characteristics of both a marketing and purchasing cooperative, putting it squarely in between the two.

A local-food cooperative markets the products of their members for a small administrative fee. Typically, the cooperatives do not keep an inventory, meaning that they don't purchase the products from their members and then sell them off. Instead, they're the facilitators of a transaction, like an enzyme. Local-food cooperatives will provide additional services to stimulate sales that a single producer wouldn't be able to do, like an online store or delivery, and they'll keep a physical location for centralizing the products of the cooperative, like a warehouse or storefront. Fresh Food Hub provides all of these local-food cooperative services to their providers, but their providers aren't the business's members – the customers are.

A purchasing cooperative aggregates products that a certain target market of a region is interested in. The combined economic power of these customers allows the cooperative to buy in bulk, negotiate down prices, and provide a centralized place to sell a variety of products. Purchasing cooperatives are just like any other merchandiser, but membership comes with discounts or perks that other for-profits don't offer. Fresh Food Hub began in 2015 in order to provide the residents of Norwood and surrounding areas with a single centralized location to shop for food produced by hobbyists, family farms, and professionals in the community. While they're technically a purchasing cooperative because their membership's main interest in the co-op is as a customer, FFH only does limited purchasing. The majority of the groceries they offer aren't inventory of FFH, rather they're inventory of the producer who provided it to be sold at the FFH marketplace. This puts FFH in a strange stance when compared to other cooperatives. Their purpose, perks, and membership are the same as any other purchasing cooperative, yet they lack the primary business activity which purchasing cooperatives form to provide – purchasing. Other than this exception, FFH performs on the customer end like any other local-food co-op. Anybody can buy food from Fresh Food Hub, though membership comes with a 7.5% discount. Their membership discount is just that, a discount. Unlike other purchasing cooperatives such as REI or Monte Vista Cooperative, their members save that money instantly upon purchase, it does not come back as a dividend at a later date. Fresh Food Hub is similar to Western Colorado Beekeepers Association in that they do not distribute dividends or refunds, yet they are still legally a cooperative. All profits are put back into the cooperative or used to support community events and workshops. Community is an important focus of FFH; from their 'Fresh Ideas' blog about the food they sell, to free yoga they offer four days a week, there are plenty of examples of FFH providing as much benefit for their community as a business can.

Fresh Food Hub combines these two cooperative models to include the best of each. FFH partners with +34 producers within a 120-mile range of Norwood to sell their products on FFH's website or at the storefront. Their producers supply apples, juices and ciders, bread, coffee, eggs, beef, milk, pork, hemp, fruits, vegetables, preservatives, seeds, cheese, honey, soaps, herbs, and tea among other goods. These items are delivered to FFH by the producers in the producer's custom packaging. Because FFH doesn't buy the product, the producer gets to choose the price. FFH simply shelves them and adds a barcode sticker with their own small marketing fee incorporated, transferring the producer's desired revenue back to them after the sale. These methods of supply give FFH a large network of producers from which to source goods with incredibly low inventory costs and limited inventory risk. Having the customers play the part of members instead of the producers gives FFH a dependable customer base that a regular marketing cooperative wouldn't enjoy due to the time and/or membership dues that the consumer-members invest in the business. Fresh Food Hub has managed to combine the ease of supply and distribution of a marketing cooperative with the dependable purchasing base and diversified consumer pool of a purchasing cooperative – the most favorable perks of both cooperative models.

The benefits of membership are standard to a purchasing cooperative, but the types of membership offered are more varied. The standard purchasing membership is called the Community Membership and costs $12.50 every month, which pays off if a member spends over $41 in groceries at FFH every week. The other membership types are free but come with monthly requirements for volunteering. Work-Trade Member is the unpaid version of Community Membership, trading the $12.50 monthly obligation for a minimum six hours of monthly volunteering. Shop-Supporter Members are for businesses who buy wholesale from FFH. They're free like Work-Trade, and require +6 hours of volunteering every month, but receive additional discounts on wholesale orders for their establishments in exchange.

Fresh Food Hub's unique membership structure among Coloradan local-food cooperatives says volumes about why Fresh Food Hub was started. The members of a cooperative make up the population who shared a common issue before the cooperative began and in every other case, those people are farmers. However, this is a local-food cooperative of consumers that seek out producers, whereas most local-food cooperatives are producers seeking out consumers. That FFH has had success with this business model shows how dedicated a town can be in their resolve to avoid corporate food and eat locally.

Farmers' markets

Cooperative farmers' markets are also local-food cooperatives; they don't use delivery rights, they facilitate a marketplace to connect growers to customers, and they make profit by taking a percentage of a producing member's sales. In addition to local-food, farmers' markets are likely to be multi-stakeholder cooperatives because they require an administrative team with a wider range of skills to operate. Procuring public (or private) space to stage the market, setting up tables, gates, and parking, getting the producing member's goods to the event, advertising for, and staffing the market necessitates a small army of people who are often specialized in doing one or two of the many tasks. All these people, regardless of what role they perform, are different types of stakeholders in the co-op, and are likely to visit a stand or two at the market, doing business with the co-op as a customer or customer-member, which is where the definition of multi-stakeholder cooperatives comes from.

This isn't as common in non-farmers' market local-food cooperatives because not as many of the people that are considered their 'stakeholders' do business with, or are members of, the co-op. Farmers' markets tend to draw out entire communities while online local-food cooperatives will attract the niche consumers who are particularly interested in buying goods that originated in the region.

The Future of Local-food Cooperatives

The fact that local-food cooperatives arose in the response to a shift in American taste rather than in the response to the growing domination of corporate agriculture strongly suggests that their continued existence is contingent on Americans desiring homegrown products. Local-food cooperatives survive because a sect of the population is willing to pay extra to know that their food comes from their community. If the attitude towards the origination of food swings back towards apathy, as it was for the majority of the 20th century, or if an economic recession robs their customers of the ability to pay premium prices, local-food cooperatives will disappear regardless of how well they have managed to compete with corporate agriculture in restaurants and grocery stores.

Chapter 7

New-generation Cooperatives

New-generation cooperatives were formed in the 1980s and 1990s in the belief that their model would address the issue of depressed farm income by employing value-adding processing; the increased profit margin could be kicked back to the co-op members, essentially capturing a larger revenue per acre for the farmers than they would receive selling the raw materials to a corporate processor.

Of the seven agricultural cooperative forms, new-generation cooperatives can be the most difficult to understand for someone new to the concept of cooperatives. New-generation co-ops have operations, legal contracts, and value propositions that are more complex than those in other kinds of co-ops. The appeal of new-generation co-ops are, essentially, that they kick back profits from value adding activity performed on a farmer's raw crop.

In corporate agriculture, the journey from raw crop to processed good might go through several companies that specialize in one of the steps, or through one company that does all the steps themselves. Delivery rights aren't exclusive to new-generation co-ops; non-cooperative companies in agriculture also use delivery contracts to ensure that they can depend on a certain volume of supply to process. A farmer in north east Nebraska, where the hills roll and windmills spin, owns a mid-sized operation and contracts with Flour Inc., a C corporation, based out of Omaha. A C corporation is the legal form of a business where the business and its owners are taxed

in succession on the business's profits; the stereotypical 'big business' is a C-corp. In the contract, he promises to harvest 33,000
bushels of wheat, around 1,000 acres worth, for Flour Inc. this season. In return, Flour Inc. promises to pay him $300,000 for his entire
harvest. After harvest season is over, Flour Inc. pays the farmer and
takes the wheat to one of their grain elevators near Omaha. Over
the winter, they pound that wheat into flour at their processing facilities. The flour is packaged with the Flour Inc. logo, and sold wholesale to the grocery stores that Flour Inc. has contracts with. Flour
Inc. pockets the difference between the $300,000 they paid for the
farmer's wheat, and the revenue they made when selling those
33,000 bushels of wheat as flour.

A farmer in northern Colorado also grows wheat. They contract with a processor, but the processor is a new-generation cooperative instead of a C corporation. He, too, agrees to sell 33,000
bushels for $300,000. The new-generation co-op takes the wheat to
an elevator outside of Denver where it is pounded into flour over the
winter. It's packaged with the logo of the co-op, or a partner of the
co-op, and sold wholesale to grocery stores that the co-op, or affili-
ate company, has their own delivery contracts with. The profit that is
accumulated between buying the wheat for $300,000 and selling
that amount of wheat as flour goes back to the co-op. The co-op
pockets a proportion of the profit to grow the business, but a certain
amount is set aside to go back to the farmer, who is a co-op member, as a dividend. This is the allure of a new-generation co-op; the
farmer makes money when he sells his crops, but also when the co-
op sells the goods it made with his crops. It isn't an incredible
amount – the farmer still makes the lion's share of his money off

selling the raw materials, but the kickback from his harvest being processed is practically free money – and it is free money that usually comes at the time when a farmer most wants a large cash influx. These dividends aren't paid out annually like in other kinds of co-ops; they accumulate over the farmer's career and are paid out when the farmer hits retirement age. A single year's worth of dividend might not make an impact on a member's economic wellbeing, but after 20-30 years of membership, the accrued dividends can be an impressive sum of money and a staple of the famer's retirement finances.

An interesting point about new-generation cooperatives is that although they exist to get farmers more revenue than they would selling to an agricultural corporation, they're often just as big as, if not bigger than, agricultural corporations. The standard bellicose attitude towards big food in America is bellicose in part because it is assumed that they put small to medium farms out of business. If 'big food' is a co-op made of small to medium farms, does that change the anti-big-business sentiment towards it?

Western Sugar Cooperative

Charles Boettcher was a wealthy Colorado businessman around the turn of the 20th century. He is still known today for his family's philanthropy, including the Boettcher Concert Hall, the Denver Botanical Gardens, and the Boettcher Mansion. The Great Western Sugar Company came from a late-career interest of the tycoon in sugar beets. In 1906, the Fort Morgan facility was built with a capacity to process 600 tons of sugar beets per day. By 1916, there were four plants processing 2,924 tons every day across Colorado, Montana, Wyoming, and Nebraska. Boettcher's company was sold to another Colorado businessman, Billy White, in 1967, who sold it again seven years later to the Hunt Brothers organization, an oil family from Texas famous for their successful investment into silver. Western Sugar was then tied into the silver trade, controlling 21 million silver contracts.

Western Sugar would go on to be used as a tool for the Hunt Brother's silver aspirations as a purchasing entity of a further 30 million ounces of silver. With their use of the Great Western Sugar Company in this manner came the possible violation of corner marketing laws, so the Hunt Brothers ceased use of Western Sugar and sold it to a British sugar firm in 1985, who renamed the company to simply 'Western Sugar Company'.

Over the next 15 years, the volatile market would pressure the English firm, Tate and Lyle, to sell their recently purchased American sugar company. The 2002 buyer of Western Sugar Company was a Colorado cooperative formed in 2000 called Rocky Mountain Sugar Growers Cooperative. Between June 2000 and April 2002, Rocky Mountain Sugar Growers Cooperative authorized over $30,000,000 in patron preferred stock in order to raise the funds to facilitate the purchase of Western Sugar Company.

The Western Sugar Cooperative was formed in late April 2002 after the purchase of Western Sugar Company by Rocky Mountain Sugar Growers Cooperative, and subsequent merging of the two entities. The private sugar hobby of Charles Boettcher had transformed into the 85th largest agricultural cooperative in the

United States by revenue, 5th largest sugar cooperative in the nation, and most valuable cooperative in Colorado.

Today, the Western Sugar Cooperative operates similarly to grain elevators like Flagler Cooperative, or Roggen Farmers Elevator Association; they buy and process the goods of their farmer members. The list of products from WSC is short and sweet: sugar, light brown sugar, dark brown sugar, powdered sugar, and fine granulated sugar. They also sell the co-products, which is everything from the sugar beets that isn't turned into sugar, as feed for livestock. From these few items, WSC regularly hits $350 million in sales every year – 5% of the domestic market share.

Annually, over 1,000 employees produce more than 10 million hundred-weights of sugar and serve 140 food processor, food service, and grocery retail customers. Their cohort of farmer members recently rose to over 1,000, including 4th and 5th generation growers who have been working for the company since the times of Boettcher.

Membership within the cooperative is very straightforward. Buying Patron Preferred Shares entitles a member to raise an acre of beets per share. The shareholder has a contractual agreement with the cooperative to deliver on their acreage. This contract also sets the standards for how much the shareholder will be payed for the beets delivered, which is further defined as the percentage of sugar content per ton of beet. The obligations of each party in the Shareholder Agreement are the delivery of a certain amount of product on part of the farmer, and payment of a certain rate for that amount on part of the cooperative. Through this deal, farmers can count on selling all of their sugar crop, and the cooperative can count on having a constant and familiar supply of raw sugar beet to process – the top two uncertainties for each were it not for the relationship.

The cooperative also has common shares, which are used for voting purposes, at the price of $1 per share. When becoming a new member, a household must buy one share of common stock in order to receive voting privileges, and at least one Patron Preferred Share in order to grow sugar for the cooperative. These limited Patron Preferred Shares are already owned by existing members, meaning that to join the cooperative, one must buy another member out, or reduce the volume of that existing member's delivery rights.

WSC can scale the Patron Preferred Shares to reflect the current state of their operations. If WSC expands their processing volume, they may either issue more Patron Preferred stock, or adjust how much acreage one share reflects, ensuring they don't over or under purchase from their members if the company's capabilities fluctuate.

Today, about 135,000 base acres represent the number of Patron Preferred Shares. The value of a Patron Preferred Share would logically be just above the profit of the acreage that the share grants – if WSC's price nets $600 in profit for an acre of sugar beets, a farmer wouldn't take anything less than $600 in selling that share – unless they were immediately retiring, or closing/suspending operations.

In keeping up with the times, WSC has recently focused heavily on sustainability. They claim to have reduced water use by

37%, fossil fuel use by 47%, greenhouse gas emissions by 80%, and the environmental impact of chemical applications by over 99%. Their efforts have been recognized for this through an award in sustainable baking, and they contribute to advancing farming efficiency by investing $350,000 annually into university and government research. These practices aren't exactly organic, and WSC never claims to be. They're a company that calls themselves "pro GMO" because of the environmental sustainability GMOs allow. Their position on GMOs isn't the only possibly controversial stance they hold publicly. WSC is also very pro-sugar and produces recipes, infographics, reports, charts, and other material detailing the upsides of a diet with caloric sweeteners (versus one with artificial sweeteners).

What's curious about The Western Sugar Cooperative is that although it is the largest and highest earning cooperative in Colorado, it is also one of the easiest to understand. Farmers promise a certain about of sugar beets to the cooperative, who promises a certain price for those beets. The cooperative takes those beets and turns them into a few variations of sugar, then sells it to food-related businesses, sending some of the profits back to the members. That's it. Even the contract between farmer and business is easy to understand, one Patron Preferred Share means one acre of sugar beets and has the value of the profit on that acre. One common share per member is the voting structure. Their simplicity in operations refutes any notion that a cooperative needs to be complex to maximize revenue – think Agfinity – as Western Sugar Cooperative has created an empire from a single vegetable.

Roggen Farmers Elevator Association

Roggen Farmers Elevator Association is the grain empire of northeastern Colorado. From Commerce City in Denver, to north of Fort Collins, and further east than Fort Morgan, then down south to Limon, this agricultural cooperative operates across over 5,000 square miles of the Colorado high plains – an area larger than the state of Connecticut. It wasn't always this way. Roggen Farmers Elevator Association started in the city of its namesake, Roggen, Colorado, in 1955. Like many other agricultural cooperatives, it formed to give its farmer members a leverage against larger corporations in marketing their products. Grain transport, storage, marketing, and distribution remains its top business function.

Expansion started in the late 1970s – expansion in both storage capacity and regions served. In 2019, Roggen had five elevator locations and a bin capacity of 5.6 million bushels, up almost 2 million bushels since in 1998.

Membership in RFEA looks a lot like the membership structure of other producer-centered agricultural cooperatives. 125 producer members make up the voting body, and the co-op averages 100 active voters per ballot. The 125 producing members act as 'RFEA marketing firm's' suppliers and pay $500 when joining. Patron members do not produce for the cooperative. They can't vote, but only pay $50 to join. Benefits for these 600 patron members include the end-product of RFEA's new-generation machine: dairy, eggs, and flour. These end products come from RFEA's network of value adding endeavors; often times these enterprises are clever symbiotic partnerships formed between the cooperative and other businesses in the areas.

Commerce City Grain is a firm in northeast Denver that has a capacity for storing over 5.3 million bushels. The firm is a partnership between RFEA and Ardent Mills, a flour and grain company that markets to household. This 50/50 ownership between the cooperative and the B2C (Business to Consumer) represents the balance between the supplier and the demander. RFEA needs a place to store its members product, and a buyer to purchase that product. Ardent Mills needs a reliable, trustworthy supply of grain and a place to store it while it awaits processing. Both benefit, theoretically, equally from Commerce City Grain as these elevators address the needs of each.* Commerce City Grain is no side project for RFEA either – 70% of their activity is grain trade through this subsidiary.

Another 50/50 partnership that RFEA has is with Opal Foods, an egg producer. In 2019, a $7.5 million feed mill was completed in Roggen of which the two businesses share ownership. The feed mill is the exclusive provider for Opal Foods' chicken farm in Roggen.

Watkins Grain LLC, in Watkins, CO, was fully acquired by RFEA in 2016 for good reason; they focused on exporting internationally. For a single-state cooperative like Roggen Farmers Elevator Association, global trade may have at one time seemed

---

* Even if the economic benefit between the two isn't equal relative to each's overall finances, a 50/50 partnership speaks to the cooperation between the two in decision making, fiscal investment, and necessity of the relationship.

unobtainable, but acquiring a private firm with international relation-ships, like Watkins, is a sensible way to begin exporting grain.

With all of RFEA's entrepreneurial savviness, it's unsurpris-ing that they keep a sharp eye on their finances. Grain trading is an industry with small margins and large volumes; it's the penny stock of the agricultural industry. This is the biggest frustration for RFEA. Unlike other businesses, even in the agricultural world, they're una-ble to grow their revenue by R&D – they can't easily 'release' a new grain or upgrade their products; they're not a tech company that can go from $2 million to $200 million in revenue from the same office building. The best way for them to expand their revenue is to expand their grain empire's physical area and maximum capacity, and, as they've demonstrated, ensure as much of their member's grain is guaranteed to sell as possible through direct partnerships with other businesses. Even then, the numbers are tight. Roggen Farmers Ele-vator Association recently had a year where they closed $60 million in revenue. Their profit on that was $922,000 – a profit margin of ~1.5%.

A point of pride for Roggen Farmers Elevator Association is their ability to pay out the lifetime dividends accumulated by their farmers. Instead of paying out dividends every year, RFEA's mem-bers have their equity deferred until they reach a certain age, usually between 50 and 60. Some agricultural cooperatives get a bad image because they're unable to generate enough cash to pay back the deferred equity to their members once their members 'retire'. Unlike those cooperatives, RFEA treats this deferred equity as a liability in their accounting, which ensures that financial decision-making re-spects the dividends. At the end of the day, RFEA's purpose is to provide a monetary benefit to its members. The idealistic coopera-tive values in this book matter only to the core voting members – to everyone else, cash is king.

"We run [this] business like a private business, we just hap-pen to be owned by farmers."

-Keith DeVoe, CEO

Sweet Grass Cooperative

Sweet Grass Cooperative began as many agricultural coop-eratives do. Seven San Luis Valley ranches and farms met in March of 2010 to address a problem that each faced. Providing a con-sistent, year-round supply of genuine grass-fed beef raised by the values of sustainable and self-aware ranching.

Their membership has grown since 2010 to 25 members in 2019, five of which form the cooperative's board. There is no cost to join the cooperative, however there are delivery rights that ensure members are active providers. Their beef can be found anywhere between Denver and Albuquerque.

Sweet Grass is a marketing cooperative and market via word of mouth, partnerships, and searching out local grocers and butch-ers. While some new-generation cooperatives use their delivery rights like stock within the cooperative, and heavily regulate the tran-sition of rights between members, Sweet Grass encourages mem-bers to shift volume requirements among one another to make fulfilling overall cooperative quantity demands as painless as possible. Each member, regardless of size of operation, receives the same price per head to ensure solidarity in the co-op and to keep the team together.

The actual business entity of Sweet Grass is sustained by variable fees charged to members when they sell to processors. These fees pay for the upkeep, taxes, administration, and the future designs of the co-op.

In 2020, Sweet Grass's primary functions were providing high quality beef to the local region and regenerating the environment in which they operate. In the future, they plan to expand the values that they formed around by diversifying the people, places, and things that are benefited by these primary functions. Becoming bird-friendly and enacting strict feeding protocol are ways they can improve their ecological impact. Developing their value-adding services to the co-op's business activities, meat processing, will expand the co-op's convenience to members and control over humane treatment. Sweet Grass is also looking to expand their apprenticeship program, a curriculum that helps ease young adults into ranching, regardless of education or background.

The principles of Sweet Grass go much deeper than face-value concepts. Sweet Grass's true differentiation lies in the peripherals of their main business activities. Their vision is to have all factors of the triple bottom line, people, profit, and planet, aligned with socially, economically, and ecologically sustainable animal agriculture.

Humane treatment of cattle during raising and slaughtering is necessary to Sweet Grass ranchers. Because cattle raising is the passion, expertise, and oftentimes heritage of SGC's ranchers, it's impossible for them to be apathetic about their cattle right from birth to the last minutes of their lives. The daily direct contact these ranchers have with their cattle forms a bond between the owner and the herd. SGC ranchers provide the most natural life possible for a cow in the San Luis Valley: being pasture-raised on a grass and forage environment, working with calm and patient ranchers, and their facilities are built with natural cattle instincts in mind. SGC ranchers show care and respect to their cattle through these low-stress methods. Sweet Grass ranchers also work with processors to ensure cattle are being slaughtered humanely by ensuring that processors are as up-to-date and benign as modern practices allow.

The economics of the beef industry are the most frustrating aspect of ranching for Sweet Grass Cooperative. Their strict sustainable ranching methods are more beneficial to society than 'Big Beef' but come at the expense of heighten costs per head and less volume. Sweet Grass is in the grass-fed beef market, thus doesn't have to directly compete with mass-beef producers, who contend over which of them can sell at the lowest price, though this doesn't mean that the grass-fed industry is squeaky clean ethically. International meat packers can legally take grass-fed beef from Uruguay and label it as "product of the USA", so long as the carcasses of these South American-raised cattle are cut into smaller portions at facilities the United States, making profits by paying South American farmers pennies on the dollars that they would pay American ranchers for the same product. The Country of Origin Label law (COOL) was repealed for beef and pork in 2015, allowing producers to exclude any indication of country of origin on packaging, which means that customers have absolutely no way of knowing if "product of the USA" grass-fed beef goods are from American ranches or not. This unethical behavior is supported by B2C marketplaces like Whole Foods who have used this cheap imported meat to force down contracts with American ranchers by 40%. Sweet Grass is indirectly affected by this; their primary commercial buyer is Panorama Meats, who aggregates, packages, and markets meat that is certified "Born and Raised in the USA", a program that clears the ambiguity of meat origin since the repeal of COOL. Panorama sells to Whole Foods, Abundant Harvest Organics, and other premium product marketplaces, thus competes with the international importers.

Sweet Grass's customers are diverse; while Panorama is their main commercial buyer, there are many local markets and butcher shops that purchase their beef. Salazar Natural Meats is a butcher shop that sells Sweet Grass beef both at their store in Manassa and online. Sweet Grass Cooperative also works with La Monta Vida Cooperative, a food co-op in New Mexico. The menus of local restaurants in the San Luis Valley sport beef dishes made from Sweet Grass cattle; you could eat a cheeseburger in Saguache cooked from the meat of a cow born and raised not 10 miles away. Their partnership with La Monta Vida Cooperative is a fantastic example of agricultural cooperatives supporting other agricultural cooperatives. On the supplier side of Sweet Grass, their ranchers buy hay grown in the San Luis Valley from farmers who are members of the Monte Vista Cooperative.

Modern animal agriculture has come under fire for being terrible for the environment. In the United States, the meat industry is responsible for 3.3% of all carbon emissions, and 38% of methane pollution.[42] Sweet Grass is actively working to combat this. Cows produce methane, which can't be captured and returned to soil, but Sweet Grass's soil restoration methods can take carbon dioxide, which is responsible for 83% of all US carbon pollution, and use it to re-enrich the depleted earth. When soil is damaged by overuse, it loses its capacity to store carbon. By allowing cattle to graze naturally, as they did for thousands of years, the soil of Sweet Grass's pastures is reinforced with nutrients that help it store carbon again.

Based on this triple bottom line business model, Sweet Grass Cooperative makes all buying and selling decisions by asking four questions:

1. Who does it benefit the most?

2. How will it have a positive effect on our environmental restoration?

3. How does it help the community?

4. Is it economically viable?

By making decisions that satisfy the concerns addressed by these questions, Sweet Grass Cooperative will continue to succeed in their mission to improve the triple bottom line by practicing sustainable, humane, and purposeful ranching.

---

[42] Center for Sustainable Systems, University of Michigan. 2018. "Carbon Footprint Factsheet." Pub. No. CSS09-05.

New-generation Co-op v. C Corporation

The differences between 'family farming' and 'corporate farming' are not as pronounced as one may believe. While it is true that small farms are family-owned, it's also true that many medium and large farms are family-owned as well. In fact, some of the biggest farms in the United States are owned by families, not corporations. Around 86% of all farms in the US are classified as family farms; farms owned by corps make up less than 9%.[43] This disparity also matches the amount of acreage owned by each type; family farms own a total of 541 million acres while corporations hold 140 million. This difference is a better representation of the true difference in power within the farming industry – family farms own 3.9 acres for every 1 that a business does. The term 'corporate farming' is more related to the effects that corporate processors have on American farms, rather than the idea that "corporate farms" are in direct competition with family farmers.

The true weight of corporate agriculture lies in the level above the farm in the secondary sector. This is the industry that has condensed over the past 100 years into mega-corporations that have the power to drive down prices among American farmers. It is family businesses, not family farms, that have disappeared in the revolution of mass food processing. The family farms that once sold to local bakers, butchers, restaurants, and grocers still exist, but now

---

[43] National Agricultural Statistics Service. (2019). 2017 Census of Agriculture (pp. 1-820, Rep.). DC: USDA.

they sell to corporations, and new-generation cooperatives, in lieu of the brick and mortar shops that were once their customers.

The biggest US companies that make up, or drive, corporate agriculture are Cargill, which is one of the largest privately-owned businesses in on the planet, NestleUSA, Archer Daniels Midland, which is the third biggest food processor in the world, and Sysco. The largest new-generation cooperative in the United States is CHS Inc. with a 2019 revenue of $32.7 billion; the second largest, A Kansas dairy co-op, drops down to $14.8 billion.[44] Of Cargill's total $115 billion in 2019 revenue, $32.5 billion came from food, not far off of CHS Inc.'s $19.2 billion in 2019 food sales. Within the food and beverage industry, new-generation cooperatives take spots 16, 26, and 84 out of the top 100 companies.[45]

New-generation cooperatives might not be as big as the C corporations they compete with, but they're big all the same – enough to enjoy some of the hallmarks of power stereotypical of C corporations. In St. Paul, Minnesota is the only stadium in the nation named after an agricultural co-op, CHS Field. Land O'Lakes, another MN new-generation co-op, isn't the namesake of US Bank Stadium in Minneapolis, but they were the third largest founding partner in the arena's construction.

---

[44] USDA Rural Development. (2018). Agricultural Cooperative Statistics 2017. Agricultural Cooperative Statistics 2017. USDA Rural Development. Retrieved from https://www.rd.usda.gov/files/publications/SR81_CooperativeStatistics2017.pdf

[45] BNP Media. (2019). 2019 Top 100 Food & Beverage Companies. Retrieved from https://www.foodengineeringmag.com/2019-top-100-food-beverage-companies

The food processors that are headquartered in Colorado are small, private, regional manufacturers. Many of the large country-wide brands have plants in the state like Cargill, Shamrock Foods, and MillerCoors Brewing, and contribute billions to Colorado's economy. The competition for RFEA and Western Sugar comes from these out-of-state companies.

The word 'corporation' has steadily gained strong negative connotations in every industry, while the word 'cooperative' stirs sentiments of a relic from your grandpa's era. This connotation of cooperatives being old, slow, and out-of-date is damaging for every form of an agricultural cooperative – except for the new-generations. New-generation cooperatives are just as competitive, powerful, regionally dispersed, and revenue-focused as C corporations, but the name 'cooperative' and fact that they're owned by farmers tends to defang them on the surface.

What's in a Name?

Western Sugar Corporation versus Western Sugar Cooperative. To the average American, one sounds like a progressive, farmer-friendly, environmentally conscientious remnant of the 1950's and the other sounds like a greedy, profit-focused entity that desires to build a monopoly over sugar in the west by buying out financially vulnerable family farms.

Whether corporations in agriculture are 'evil' or not is a matter of opinion on economic policy. But, if they *were* evil, would the cooperative articles of incorporation spare new-generation co-ops from the same characterization? If the Western Sugar Cooperative was sold to a private equity firm, or a wealthy investor, and became the Western Sugar Corporation overnight, does the loss of farmer ownership affect the fundamental ethics of the company? In this case, the board of directors of Western Sugar would now report to a team of portfolio managers instead of to a voting body of farmer-owners. That a voting body would make more ethical decisions about operation than a council of oligarchs is an assumption that an American would make unconsciously, but it may not be the case in every situation. As the CEO of Roggen Farmer Elevators Association said, "We run business like a private business, we just happen to be owned by farmers."

Chapter 8

Multi-stakeholder Cooperatives

In theory, multi-stakeholder cooperatives are made up of members who interact with the cooperative in different capacities. Imagine a co-op where the farmers, processors, distributors, truckers, buyers, and administrators are all members of the business. USDA economist Dr. Ling's idea is that by engaging the entire supply chain of a co-op in membership with the co-op, the business becomes "a framework for mutual adaptation and for multi-party, multi-stage credible contracting among members only when they deal with each other in attending to the cooperative's business."[46]

Memberships in agricultural cooperatives are predominantly sorted into producers and consumers. Purchasing cooperatives are made of consuming members, marketing cooperatives are made of producing members, and local-food cooperatives oftentimes have both. An unexplained element of Dr. Ling's multi-stake cooperatives is how membership works when additional stakeholders are added as a new class of member. Where does the voting power lie? How are dividends distributed? What benefits would a 'logistics member' like a trucker or administrator get for being a member of the cooperative?

In the real world, or at least in Colorado, there aren't any multi-stakeholder cooperatives in the way Dr. Ling describes it; it doesn't seem to be a practical, or applicable, method of running an agricultural

---

[46] Ling, C. (2012). The Many Faces of Cooperatives. Rural Cooperatives, 79(6), 24-29.

cooperative. Instead, the closest examples of multi-stake holder co-operatives are co-ops that engage the greatest number of their stakeholder types in business or membership. These cooperatives do so by design but not on purpose – they simply happen to attract the most stakeholder types through their efforts to appeal to an entire city.

Colorado Farm and Art Market

Once upon a time, small producers and family farms in Colorado Springs were not able to sell their goods at local farmers' markets. They were either denied access to the events altogether because of their small size or were dominated by large out-of-state vendors who swept the same markets with a flood of products. Fed up with being overlooked or overshadowed, these agriculturalists formed Colorado Farm and Art Market in early 2004.

Since the beginning, the goal of CFAM was to foster a marketplace for a truly local list of vendors. Today, over 40 of those vendors fill their year-round schedule. The cooperative runs two days per week from June to October, seasonally during the December holidays, and once weekly from January to May. The 100%-Coloradan catalogue of items that show up throughout the year ranges from produce and baked goods to candles, scarves, and toothpaste.

Membership is centered around producers. Of the 40 vendors, the majority of them are members of the cooperative. CFAM allows non-member vendors, 'guest vendors', to sell at their market, but it's economically beneficial to join up if a family intends to appear on multiple days throughout the year because all vendors at CFAM pay a flat rate per day to have a table, plus 5% of their sales, and members receive a discounted table rate.

Like in other cooperatives, membership also comes with the right to vote. Voting at CFAM happens once per year at an annual meeting where several issues are resolved. First is the board of the cooperative. Throughout the year, the co-op is run by a board of elected members who make the day-to-day decisions of operation, and also craft long-term strategic goals. Another decision made at these meetings is what to do with the cooperative's profits from the last year. CFAM profits from membership fees, day table rates, and a 5% siphoning of vendor sales. These profits could go back to the vendor members, be invested in the cooperative, or be split between both. Members also weigh in on the business's long-term trajectory at the annual meeting. Editing the bylaws of the cooperative and proposing future business goals are a few examples of what some of these policy ballot items might pertain.

A policy decision that was once on the voting ballot was the business form itself. The cooperative structure makes sense for a local farmers' market, but so does the nonprofit structure. Once, CFAM members were considering a switch to the nonprofit form in order to receive access to grants that are specific to nonprofits. The motion failed – the sentiment of ownership that comes with being a cooperative member was too strong to overpower an economic incentive. The members of CFAM would rather stick to being a true cooperative than switch for the sake of access to money. On the other side of the co-op, the board members do not have many quarrels about being a cooperative. Membership turnover can get burdensome for agricultural cooperatives, especially small ones with little administrative power. If the producer vendors of CFAM rotated in and out every year, the board members would push for a switch to nonprofit as the high turnover would make it incredibly hard for CFAM to keep legal compliance with the government. Because CFAM keeps over 75% of its vendors every year, the amount of paperwork generated by the coming and going of a minority of the membership population is manageable by their administrative team.

Colorado Farm and Art Market competes with other farmers' markets in the region, but they are the only cooperative. In the farmers' market world, there are two segments over which rival organizations can compete: for customers and for vendors. Recently, CFAM has seen growth in sales and a steady customer base, yet they have been losing vendors to these competing farmers' markets. Some vendors don't like the idea of membership; they don't want to commit to one organization because it makes them feel like they're giving up the mobility of finding the 'sweet spot' of whichever farmers' market is doing particularly well each season. There's also been some frustrations among the members in regard to how the cooperative is being run; if two members disagree on a decision, or don't agree with each other on politics or strategy, it's easy for one or both to leave CFAM and go to another organization where interaction between the vendors isn't a large part of doing business.

CFAM has not been idle with these issues. They've taken steps to optimize the funnel for vendor members' concerns to reach the ears of the board members. They've also been working to promote the more obscure membership type – the consumer member. Consumer membership has been around in the past, yet it hasn't been effectively advertised or has lacked compelling enough incentives for repeat customers to take an interest. Now, CFAM is building out the consumer membership. They're revisiting the perks and considering giving them voting power. An interesting thought about their future is the potential flipping of power within the cooperative. If vendor members continue to leave while consumer membership gains steam, CFAM might find themselves as a farmers' market made up of consumer members whose shared interest is seeking local vendors to buy from and facilitating market concentration.

Foodshed Alliance

Foodshed Alliance was a Salida cooperative founded in mid-2007 and dissolved on the last day of 2018. Foodshed Alliance is now a nonprofit corporation, founded in mid-2018 and undergoing steady growth. The story of this cooperative is one that demonstrates both the upsides and downsides of the cooperative business form, and provides a real-life example of when a different type of structure, a nonprofit corporation, is better at delivering a benefit to its 'members' than a cooperative.

Foodshed Alliance formed around the need for the local growers of Salida to more easily reach the local market. Instead of offering a storefront or online delivery service like other Colorado marketing co-ops, however, they decided that the function of the co-op would be to host farmers' markets. These markets are quite intricate, which necessitates the economic and managerial organization that a cooperative offers. The summer markets are in Salida and Buena Vista and run on Saturdays from June to October. The winter market also runs on a handful of Saturdays across December, January, and February, but only in Salida.

In the beginning, when there were only a few producers in Salida, the cooperative model worked perfectly. The ownership in the business that membership brings was a great selling point when pitching the concept of a co-op-run farmers' market to prospective members, and the economic parameters of a cooperative provided intrinsic insurance against being scammed or duped. From the first season in 2007, the farmers' market grew and changed through democratic means. Soon, their great business practices and the steady growth of the farmers' market began to speak for itself. Throughout central Colorado, Foodshed Alliance developed a positive reputation for delivering quality farmers' markets in a friendly manner.

Now that they were able to recruit producers by touting benefits that went beyond the advantages of membership, there was to be a reassessment of the utility that a cooperative business form brought. Profits were spent on expanding the cooperative or improving its function. Money gleaned from running the markets was spent on additional tents, trucks, stands, and public spaces rather than being divided up and going back into the pockets of the members. As participation increased, so did the rate of growers dropping out. There was always some recycling of members – those who were producers with the business one year, then not the next, then possibly coming back the year after – but soon the number of vendors coming and going each year grew to a volume that made it difficult for Foodshed Alliance's administration to balance the turnover with meeting legal regulations for cooperative membership. The primary attractor of the cooperative business model, the membership, had become a legal hinderance, and the primary financial benefit of a cooperative business model, member dividends, were not being utilized. Seeing that their present method of operation was an overall cost to their business, they began to plot a transition to a nonprofit in 2017.

There are still remnants of a cooperative in the nonprofit Foodshed Alliance, most chiefly in the decision-making process. Instead of buying ownership in the business with membership fees, the new types of vendor fees give an option to buy a voting member level where they get to vote on business decisions, but that vote's source of power is not tied to ownership in the business. Other than this technical change, there aren't any distinguishable differences in the nonprofit Foodshed Alliance from its cooperative days. While vendors still rotate frequently, now Foodshed Alliance isn't bound by legal regulations to track them with such complexity as they did before. Their profit still goes back into the business and now that they're a nonprofit, it isn't taxed anymore. The sense of equality that the cooperative brought to vendor-members has been preserved by retaining a similar decision-making structure.

While this book is dedicated to describing all the fantastic ways people use the cooperative business form to solve issues in their community, it's important to state that they're not all-encompassing or infallible, and to provide examples that illustrate when co-ops are not the optimal model. For Foodshed Alliance, the cooperative model wasn't *useless*. In this case, the tenants and structure of a cooperative were their training wheels, and like training wheels, there comes a point where they're more inhibitory than useful.

Canon Co-op

What Western Colorado Beekeepers Association is to bee-keeping is more or less what Canon Co-op is to family and hobbyist agriculture. That is, Canon Co-op is less of a business whose primary goal is to provide fiscal benefits to its members and more of a club where the cooperative element acts as a skeletal structure for centralizing activities and administration around.

This isn't to suggest that there aren't commonalities between Canon Co-op and traditional agricultural cooperatives. Of Canon Co-op's three main activities, two of them seem run-of-the-mill for cooperatives across any industry: purchasing and marketing. Since Canon Co-op started in 2009, it has offered members the perks of getting in on the co-op's farmers' market stand and occasional bulk food orders – marketing and purchasing. These are both core business activities for the majority of cooperatives across the nation, but what differs Canon Co-op in this regard, and what makes them a club instead of a business, is that the co-op itself does not make any money from these transactions. In traditional cooperatives, both marketing and purchasing activities will involve, even at a miniscule level, markups when product travels across the cooperative, be it from the member to a third party or from a third party to a member. It's how the cooperative pays wages, taxes, facility upkeep, and saves for future development. The fact that Canon Co-op does not add markups is what distinguishes them as a club cooperative. There are no employees, and the board of directors volunteer their time. What little money the co-op does spend is netted from the $30 annual fees that their members pay.

Those members, about 40 in total, ranged from their 40s to 60s until recently when younger leadership within the cooperative lead a successful social media marketing campaign and recruited 20-30 new members, a chunk of those their 30s. Activity within the club cooperative reflects what one might expect from a typical club; approximately a third of members show up for meetings, which run during the growing season. Engagement with co-op events is similar, a quarter of members partake in the co-op's farmers' market stand, and the engagement with bulk ordering fluctuates with the general popularity of whatever is being ordered. All members in the club have voting rights, although one must be present at a meeting if their vote is to be counted. While these numbers might reflect low member involvement, the average member is drawn to only one or two of the three pillars – adding up to replete membership participation across bulk buying, the farmers' market, and agricultural education.

Education is the third asset that Canon Co-op offers to its members. The classes are community events open to the public but free for co-op members. The way these sessions are structured is similar to Western Colorado Beekeepers Association where 'experts' in certain aspects of agriculture, be it a member or a non-member, host an informational session about their field of expertise. Solar panels, soil ecology, cooking, and fermenting are examples of topics from the past. On top of in-person education, the co-op has a small library where members can check out books and movies – usually relating to agriculture. Another aspect of Canon Co-op's education pillar is their scholarship. The co-op has an annual scholarship that it endows to a graduating high school senior who intends to go into agriculture.

While it has seen its highs and lows, evidenced by vestigial websites and Facebook pages, Canon Co-op is clearly on a recent upswing in membership, leadership creativity, and club activity. So long as there is a healthy population of family farmers in Canon, Colorado, the Canon Co-op will remain an important community resource and unique agricultural cooperative.

What is a multi-stakeholder co-op?

In business, the idea of defining stakeholders is predicated on the assumption that if a company can figure out every single type of person, or group of persons, they have a unique interaction with, then they can optimize each interaction. Typical stakeholders are owners, employees, customers, suppliers, media, the government, creditors, investors, and the 'community'. Oftentimes, one person can represent multiple stakeholders – a Target employee fits into the stakeholder categories of employee, customer, and community. In the same way, a producing member of Western Sugar Cooperative can be a supplier, investor, and customer. This ability for a single member to be a multi-stakeholder means every single agricultural co-op is technically a multi-stakeholder co-op.

Dr. Ling's definition infers that the reason a multi-stakeholder co-op is classified as such is because there are, theoretically, membership types for each kind of stakeholder: a membership for producers, a membership for employees, a membership for customers, etc., and a member belongs to whichever class of membership that is their most predominant, or important, stakeholder type. Because this kind of membership structure doesn't exist in Colorado, the definition of a multi-stake-holder co-op must be modified to reflect the real-world co-ops that are closest in theory to Dr. Ling's definition.

The reason why multi-stakeholder cooperatives are farmers' markets is because farmers' markets have the greatest potential of shareholder diversity within their standard membership. This isn't as common in non-farmers' market local-food cooperatives because not as many of the people that are considered their 'stakeholders' do business with, or are members of the co-op. Farmers' markets tend to draw out entire communities while online local-food cooperatives tend to draw out the niche consumers who are particularly interested in buying goods that originated in the region.

The fact that they are a physical market instead of an online shop is a major contributor to this. Setting up and tearing down a farmers' market is a task that engages quite a few of the co-op's stakeholders: employees, owners, producers, the government, and the community all assist with or are involved in a weekend market. After setting it up, many of these people shop around the market for a while – they're there already, might as well browse for a bit after spending all that effort to get it running. Because farmers' markets are able to physically draw so many of their stakeholders to the event, their diversity of stakeholders represented in weekend sales is going to be far greater than in any other agricultural co-op model. The assumption from here is that the farmers' market co-op has a well-structured consumer membership so that it's a no-brainer for these stakeholders to join the co-op, thus creating a multi-stakeholder population of consumer members and making them a multi-stakeholder cooperation. In this definition of a multi-stakeholder co-op, the multi-stakeholder aspect comes from the diversity of stakeholder types within the population of consumer members, and not from a diversity of stakeholder type memberships. This definition, while not as specific in pertaining to the aspect of 'multi-stakeholder' as being important operational units of the co-op, is a better reflection of what a real-life co-op with a high diversity of stakeholders within its membership ranks would look like.

Chapter 9

Farm Production Cooperatives

The purpose of a farm production cooperative is the operation of a farm that the co-op members have pooled resources to fund. The idea behind farm production cooperatives is that, in theory, the co-op owned farm can produce at a larger scale than any one member could as an individual. It sounds like a very logical use of the cooperative model; everyone shares in the costs and the revenue; everyone profits off farm operation. The challenge with farm production cooperatives going from theory to reality is that modern farms have one of the highest start-up costs and longest break-even periods out of any type of business. To start a farm from nothing can cost several million dollars and to recuperate that investment can take decades. The most expensive aspects of modern farming are land and advanced farm equipment. The average cost of equipment to start a family-sized farm is over $750,000, while the average cost per acre of farmland in the US is $3,160.[47] The average size of a family farm in the US is 230 acres, meaning that to start a local average-sized farm somewhere between Denver and Fort Collins, where acres go for around $20,000 per, would cost $6,600,000 for land alone. The cost of working the land depends on what crop is being grown; seeding, fertilizing, and spraying an acre of corn costs

---

[47] Williamson, S. (2018, May 04). How Much $ Does It Take to Become a Farmer? Retrieved from https://www.agriculture.com/farm-management/business-planning/how-much-does-it-take-to-become-a-farmer

approximately $300, although that number is extremely sensitive to the quality of materials used.

These upfront costs are why farm production cooperatives are so rare. Membership fees aren't $20-$150 like in most cooperatives; in order to raise enough cash to purchase farmland, members must give significant contributions. Even though these fees represent, at the very least, investments into real estate that increase in value over time, convincing enough people within a community to join up to form the cooperative is much more difficult than in other cooperative types because of this high initial barrier. Perhaps in the 1800's, when land was given away for free and 'farm equipment' consisted primarily of livestock, this type of cooperative would have flourished. In the 21st century, it is inevitable that if a group of producers attempts to start a farm production co-op, a consistent challenge will be sourcing the funds to get their farm off the ground – or into it.

Poudre Valley Community Farms

There are five American farmers over 75 to every one under 25 years old. The greatest asset to these retiring farmers is their ever-increasing-in-value land, thus it is often sold to the highest bidder instead of to the future generation of farmers. This sees the majority of purchased farmland in the US being converted into non-farming uses like residential land, which removes it from the potential of production agriculture.

Poudre Valley Community Farms aims to step in and use the buying power of a cooperative to outcompete non-industry bidders at the table, thereby securing farmland for farm use. By engaging the entire community behind owning the land from which the local food supply is grown, PVCF seeks to navigate the common challenges that bar folks from starting a farm, expanding their farm, or selling their land to another farmer.

Poudre Valley Community Farms started in 2015 and in 2019 they had 104 members. The cost of membership is a one-time payment of $2,500, which the cooperative puts towards fronting loans for farmland. Member patronage is only one of the ways money is sourced; PVCF also uses donations, partner investments, and conservation easements to buy land.

Once the producing members of PVCF begin producing, the non-producing multi-stakeholder members may purchase those products with a portion of the purchase being returned as dividends, similar to how REI structures dividends. This is one form of dividend, for M-share owners. PVCF has M-shares for member-owners or households, P-shares for producing members, C-shares for companies, and I-shares for non-patronage investors.

Even with limited resources and inconsistent growth, the membership aspect of their cooperative business model allows them to mobilize quickly if opportunity arises; PVCF was able to swiftly secure a property of 109 acres in 2018 via bridge loans from community members. The cooperative must find a way to replay those loans, but the fact that a small budget, low margin business was trusted enough by their community to prove good on their vision shows the strength of the relationship cooperatives can have with their members.

Over the last four years, PVCF has purchased two properties, and has two producing members assigned to those sites. The first project began when PVCF was approached by Montava about a partnership. Montava is an agri-urban development dedicated to connecting people to their food, the environment, nature, and each other. In early 2017, PVCF, Montava, and Native Hill, the intended producer, began a discussion about implementing a 40-acre farm within the Montava residential development. Their second property is the 109-acre plot purchased via member bridge loans. The $1.3 million dollar price was covered in three ways: $275,000 of member equity, $75,000 in donations, and $950,000 of bridge loans. It's just north of Wellington, Colorado and is currently leased by Jodar Farms, an egg, pork, and chicken producer. This puts PVCF at 149 acres of their 200-acre 2020 goal, an aim sought after since 2017 when they had no land at all.

The allure of their business model is the leases that PVCF offers are competitive, long-term, and available to community farmers. Unfortunately, these competitive rates are between $150 and $200 per acre per year. Local farmland in Poudre Valley goes for $20,000 an acre to buy, so this difference makes gives PVCF a payback period of around one hundred years using rent. The goal for PVCF should be that someday the cooperative has the power to use the lease profits exclusively to buy more land, but when breaking even on the Wellington plot off of its rent will theoretically take 60 years, ($200 per acre at 109 acres makes $21,800 in rent per year towards the expense of $1.3 million) is the rent alone enough income for them?

Besides the 60-year period on breaking even, the ability to purchase additional land past the 149 acres they currently hold is entirely dependent upon recruiting additional members, public or private partnerships, and fundraising. The $275,000 of member equity spent on the Wellington plot was the majority of the collective $2,500 membership fees of the 104 members. It took Poudre Valley Community Farms four years to recruit 104 members to buy one piece of land. These members are the most enthusiastic and effortless individuals in the community to bring aboard. Finding 104 more members to purchase another plot might be aided by the producing members showing positive returns on their land leases, not to mention that the households that will move into the development at Montava represent a sufficient pool of prospective members, yet there is a limit in the Poudre Valley on potential members. Growth will be an uphill battle for PVCF.

In late 2019, PVCF was forced to confront this issue head on. In order to be debt-free from the 2018 purchase of the 109-acre Wellington property, PVCF decided to split off a third of the property, which contained the original farm house and residential structures, and sell the house/35 acres package. They retained the leftover 74 acres, on which one of their producers actively operates. This move shrunk the property's break-even period closer to 15 years, so long as they recovered the entire sum of bridge loans in the partitioning.

The good news for PVCF is that they have a great story. The only cooperatives resembling anything close to their business model are on different continents. Their unique solution to the issue of farmland distribution is the only active solution in the area. They require that producing members follow strict agrarian ethics which place land care in high regard, ensuring its longevity. Paired with 10-year leases and competitive rates, this means that there will always be a farmer sustainably working their plots. Another positive outlook for PVCF is the land they've invested in will continue to rise in value, giving the business appreciating assets.

The multi-stakeholder aspect of Poudre Valley Community Farms shines through their founding belief that the Poudre Valley community should take ownership in locally produced food. To PVCF, community means everyone – farmers, grocers, restaurants, institutions, households and individuals. Active participants in the vein of the agriculture industry, or those who are clueless about farming, anyone who lives in the Poudre Valley is a stakeholder to PVCF.

Will it Last?

Outside of the expense of land, the year-to-year cost of operating the co-op is $30,000. The 114 acres that PVCF owns earns them $22,800 per year if every acre is rented out for $200. So, on top of exhausting their investing power from the 2018 Wellington purchase, PVCF is operating at a net loss of, at best, $7,200 per year. The future of Poudre Valley Community Farms rests on the will of their leadership to maintain constant fundraising, and the continued active interest of the Poudre Valley community in the idea of community-owned farming.

Farm Production Cooperatives

Cooperatives are supposed to be practical. The reason most cooperatives form is because a group of people with a similar issue realize they could come together to start a business whose mission is to solve that shared problem. It's supposed to be logical, natural, easy. There should be fewer reasons *not* to start a co-op than reasons in support of its formation. This is true of all business; a business succeeds because there are environmental factors outside of the entity that favors its existence: affordable capital or land, manageable barriers to entry, a short break-even period. Poudre Valley Community Farms has none of these in their favor, and it will be an awfully long time before any factors swing to their side. If starting a farm production cooperative means ten years of intense battling against environmental forces to become self-sustaining, is this agricultural cooperative model even practical?

It's more practical than going it alone. A single family farm would never be able to accomplish what Poudre Valley Community Farms did by securing 114 acres of farmland within a few years so close to an urban area. If the cost to start up a family farm from scratch is over $7 million, then engaging the community around helping kickstart the project is far smarter than one or two individuals attempting to take out a lifetime's worth of loans. The fact that the best solution to confront the high price of farmland in the US, farm production cooperatives, seems impractical on paper, tells more about the state of affairs that the land market is in, rather than the legitimacy of the farm production cooperative model. The problem this type of co-op addresses is the single largest challenge in expanding the agricultural industry. The success of PVCF as one of the first US farm production cooperatives could bring about a wave of new land co-ops with similar values, practices, and members in the near future.

Chapter 10

Non-patron Member Cooperatives

Non-patron member cooperative is an oxymoron. The whole point of cooperatives is that they're made of patron members, so having a co-op whose model is designed around consolidating non-patron members is contradictory to what a cooperative is. When non-patron members invest into a co-op, they receive a certain amount of ownership in proportion of how much they invested to how much the co-op is worth. In theory, this would mean that an investor would take a share of voting power disproportionate to what the co-op members have; if one investor owns 30% of a co-op, his/her vote would account for 30% of all votes, meaning the members split the remaining 70% of voting power among themselves. States that allow non-patron members also pass laws to ensure this scenario doesn't happen by setting a minimum level of voting power for patron members or revoking the power of a non-patron member to vote altogether.

At Poudre Valley Community Farms, I-share members, the investors, do not receive representation in selecting the board of directors. Instead, their investment in the cooperative is a calculation that the co-op will grow in value without their involvement in decision making.

While USDA economist Dr. Ling defines non-patron membership as a type of cooperative model, it's more like characteristic of a larger cooperative type. In Colorado, purchasing, marketing, new-generation, local-food, and farm production cooperatives all have the option to accept non-patron members and they can control the level of involvement in voting that those members have, but they don't make the inclusion of these investors a core trait of their cooperative.

Chapter 11

Socialism in Cooperatives

A company that is owned by a collective working class sounds like socialism. In socialism, the means of making, moving, and trading wealth is owned or controlled by the workers – the money made belongs to the workers instead of to a group of private owners. The agricultural cooperatives in Colorado, especially the marketing ones, are owned, controlled, and operated by a collective working class, and any profits of the co-op go back to the workers instead of a few wealthy investors.

Socialism is widely misinterpreted or assigned false connotations everywhere in the world. This isn't helped by the fact that the world has 4-5 accepted definitions that paint the use of socialism to mean radically different things. In practice, socialism as an economic policy has meant that the job of distributing profits generated by business falls to the state, and the profits are distributed to the entire working class as a whole in the form of welfare versus to just the workers of the industry that produced the surplus. The proposed purpose of this kind of socialism is to guarantee basic needs like housing, healthcare, and education to an entire country's population.

In agricultural cooperatives, the job of distributing profits falls to the cooperative business entity while the surplus goes back to the same workers that produced the goods from which the cooperative made the profit.

The main aspect of socialism that capitalist-leaning voters take issue is the fact that the wealth is redistributed to the entire society versus to the workers that generated the wealth. Imagine if an agricultural cooperative sent dividends to every single farmer in a region instead of only the farmers in the region who belong to the cooperative. Although the farmer members still get a dividend, it is nowhere as big as it would have been were it directly tied to the amount of revenue they generated for the co-op, because they're supporting farmers outside the co-op. While both this proposed scenario and the real way a cooperative distributes dividends fit the definition of socialism, demonstrating how lose the definition can be, the distinction of *who* benefits from profit distribution and *how much* will decide if the co-op receives quiet support or outspoken denouncement. There are, after all, no cooperatives that distribute dividends to non-members.

Wealth does not return to cooperative members equally; each member receives a dividend that represents their participation in the co-op's total profit. A farmer who does twice the amount of business with their local food cooperative than another member, will receive a dividend twice as big. This is another departure from a state-enforced socialism, where the amount distributed to each citizen depends on how much they 'need'. Distributing to 'citizens' of a co-op based on the proportion of how much each generated value for the co-op is far different than distributing evenly or, like state programs, giving the most to the members who generated the least. While a cooperative fits the socialist model, its every-member-for-themself spirit of operation is truly capitalistic. A fair way to describe the role of socialism in a cooperative is that a co-op is socialist in ownership, and capitalist in distribution.

Chapter 12

The Many Faces of Cooperatives

In *The Many Face of Cooperatives*, Dr. Ling defines seven variations of the agricultural cooperative model based upon "different commodities [having] their own characteristics, and different types of cooperatives [having] their own special features."

These seven variations are marketing cooperatives, new-generation cooperatives, purchasing cooperatives, local-food co-operatives, multi-stakeholder cooperatives, farm production co-operatives, and cooperatives with non-patronage members.

The term Dr. Ling uses for classifying these, 'variation', is purposefully broad. While these terms are defined separately, and each have the word cooperative in them, they are not stand-alone terms. Although each model is supposed to have different commodities and special features, these models overlap significantly when it comes to real world application. Identifiers like "marketing" and "supply" are classifications of the primary business activities that an agricultural cooperative executes to provide value to members – meaning every agricultural co-op in Colorado falls under one of these two classes.

The best way to talk about the different types of agricultural cooperatives is similar to how you would talk about a car. At a dealership, there are classes of cars, which divide further into models, which divide further into trim levels. A Ford XLT Explorer is in the SUV class of vehicle, the Explorer model of SUV, and XLT trim level of Explorer. In the same way, Colorado Farm and Art Market is in the marketing cooperative class, a local-food cooperative model, and has the additional feature of being a multi-stakeholder co-op.

Class - Coloradan Supply Cooperatives

The difference between supply cooperatives and purchasing cooperatives is that supply cooperatives do not get the majority of their revenue from selling products. A proportion of that revenue comes from selling products, but there are also complex service-based business activities that are generating significant proportions of revenue and are independent of product vending.

Model - Coloradan Purchasing Cooperatives

In Colorado, the only model of supply-classification agricultural cooperatives are purchasing co-ops. All purchasing co-ops use membership investment to facilitate purchases on the members' be half.

Class - Coloradan Marketing Cooperatives

All Coloradan marketing cooperatives have one thing in common: they use membership investment to facilitate the sale of member goods. Be it with or without delivery rights, or to multi-stakeholder members or third parties, the root use of membership fees is to build a system to sell member goods.

Model - Coloradan Local-food Cooperatives

The local-food cooperatives do not use delivery rights, are regionally limited, and do not add value to their member's goods. Because local-food cooperatives are a model of the marketing class, they use membership investments to facilitate the sale of member goods. An exception to this is Fresh Food Hub Cooperative in Norwood, who uses member investments to facilitate the sale of goods from non-members to members. FFH's interaction with these non-members are not as a buyer; FFH does not buy local food goods to sell to their members, they simply allow non-members to sell their products to FFH members in their storefront and on their website. FFH is a local-food hub because their main business activity is aggregating and marketing the outputs from regional producers without buying those outputs as inventory.

Model - Coloradan New-generation Cooperatives

New-generation cooperatives are best characterized by having both delivering rights and value adding processes. As members of the marketing class, they use their member's investments to sell their member's outputs. Unlike local-food cooperatives and other marketing cooperatives, new-generation co-ops sell their member's crops to themselves. Profits generated when the co-op processes those outputs, which are often raw crops, into a product that can be sold to a third party with a markup. Sometimes, new-generation cooperatives will also be a purchasing cooperative – selling seed, fertilizer, and farm equipment to their growing members.

Model - Coloradan Farm Production Cooperatives

Farm production cooperatives are whatever the members make of it. In Colorado, the farm production cooperative Poudre Valley Community Farms is, at its core, a supply cooperative that uses member investments to buy land. It leases that land to producing members to farm on. Farm production co-ops will always reflect the main pillar of a supply cooperative – using member investments to buy materials, equipment and/or services on the member's behalf.

Feature - Coloradan Multi-stakeholder Cooperatives

In Colorado, multi-stakeholder cooperatives are those who have the greatest amount of stakeholder diversity within their standard memberships. These tend to be farmers' market co-ops, as – by nature – they attract the greatest variety of people within a community. Farm production cooperatives are also likely to be multi-stakeholder cooperatives because of necessity. In order to raise funding for the co-op's activities, a farm production cooperative will need to engage the entire community to invest in their endeavor.

Feature - Coloradan Non-patronage Member Cooperatives

Whenever a Coloradan co-op is considering making a large financial move, they have the ability to allow non-members to invest in their business. While this gives the investors ownership within the co-op, it does not give them voting power. This is because there are state laws that lessen or prevent the decision-making power of a non-member investor. A co-op often allows outside investment when the business is young.

People and Problems

Why agriculture? Nearly all of the most successful cooperatives in the world are in agriculture. The explosive modern industries of electronics, software, entertainment, and finance have no significant cooperatives in them. Where is the cooperative version of Apple, with millions of members aligned to design the most advanced version of electronics for themselves? Where is the movie studio made up of writers, actors, and film crews, making the movies they want, the way they want? Why don't tech businesses come together to start a cooperative cybersecurity company that's designed by the very corporations it operates to protect? All of these sound like successful business ventures – who wouldn't want to belong to an Apple cooperative?

The answer lies the two ingredients required to make a cooperative. A group of similar people and a shared problem. Perhaps the shared problem needs to have certain characteristics to be compatible with the cooperative solution. One of those characteristics is the availability, or lack thereof, of alternative solutions. Starting a cooperative is hard work – it's an entire business. If there are already a few preestablished solutions in the community, then this group of similar people will utilize those instead of coming together to make a cooperative. Apple, Sony, Google, and Microsoft have global reach. If somebody has a problem that requires a certain electronic device to solve, it's likely that there's already a company who makes it and has the capability to deliver it to them. If an actress is fed up with one studio, there are many others available for her to move to – no need to spend all that time starting a cooperative. On the other hand, maybe the problem is there, but the people aren't in a position to work together towards a solution. A cybersecurity cooperative would be immensely beneficial to thousands of tech companies. Cyber-attacks in the 21st century show that the current cybersecurity industry is still growing and there's no one infallible, domineering player in the game. The thousands of tech companies in the US all have the same problem: they need to have rock-solid cybersecurity. They are all in the same industry, so they're similar in structure. It should seem like a no brainer – a group of similar people, or companies, with a shared problem. So, where are the cybersecurity cooperatives? In this scenario, the problem is that the potential members of this cooperative aren't used to cooperation. Could you imagine Apple and Microsoft coming together and forming a cybersecurity company to protect themselves? There are just too many conflicting interests between them, the least being that one subtly benefits when the other is the victim of a cybersecurity attack because customers flee from the victim and start looking for alternatives. Many cooperatives that sound like a good idea will never be brought to fruition because the similar people can't align, or the problem already has alternative solutions.

Although, it sometimes does work. Across the world, there are instances where a group of similar people with shared problems can't find a solution as individuals and are able to overcome any competition between them. They unite, form a cooperative, and thrive off what it cultivates for them. Some of these cooperatives belong to the agricultural industry of Colorado.

AGRICULTURAL COOPERATIVES OF COLORADO

Categorization of featured co-ops by Dr. Ling's models

Co-op	MRKT	PRCH	NWGN	LOFD	MLTS	FRMP
AGFY	✓	✓	✓			
BASN		✓				
CANN	✓				✓	
CFAM	✓			✓	✓	
FLAG	✓	✓	✓			
FDSA	✓			✓	✓	
FRFH	✓	✓		✓		
HPFC	✓			✓		
MVCP		✓				
PVCF		✓			✓	✓
PVCP		✓				
PROD		✓				
RFEA	✓	✓	✓			
SWFF	✓			✓		
SWTG	✓		✓			
WCBA	✓					
WSUG	✓		✓			

AGRICULTURAL COOPERATIVES OF COLORADO

AFGY: Agfinity

BASN: Basin Co-op Inc.

CANN: Cannon Co-op

CFAM: Colorado Farm and Art Market

FLAG: Flagler Cooperative Association

FDSA: Foodshed Alliance

FRFH: Fresh Food Hub

HPFC: High Plains Food Coop

MVCP: Monte Vista Cooperative

PVCF: Poudre Valley Community Farms

PVCP: Poudre Valley Cooperative

PROD: Producer's Coop

RFEA: Roggen Farmers Elevator Association

SWFF: Southwest Farm Fresh

SWTG: Sweet Grass Cooperative

WCBA: Western Colorado Beekeepers Association

WSUG: Western Sugar Cooperative

MRKT: Marketing Cooperative

PRCH: Purchasing Cooperative

NWGN: New-generation Cooperative

LOFD: Local Food Cooperative

MLTS: Multi-stakeholder Cooperative

FRMP: Farm Production Cooperative

www.ingramcontent.com/pod-product-compliance
Lightning Source LLC
Chambersburg PA
CBHW071909200326
41519CB00016B/4545